COMEBACK SEASON

COMEBACK SEASON

My Unlikely Story *of* Friendship *with the*
GREATEST LIVING NEGRO LEAGUE BASEBALL PLAYERS

CAM PERRON with Nick Chiles

G

GALLERY BOOKS

New York   London   Toronto   Sydney   New Delhi

G

Gallery Books
An Imprint of Simon & Schuster, Inc.
1230 Avenue of the Americas
New York, NY 10020

First Gallery Books hardcover edition March 2021

GALLERY BOOKS and colophon are registered trademarks of
Simon & Schuster, Inc.

For information about special discounts for bulk purchases,
please contact Simon & Schuster Special Sales at 1-866-506-1949
or business@simonandschuster.com.

The Simon & Schuster Speakers Bureau can bring authors to
your live event. For more information or to book an event,
contact the Simon & Schuster Speakers Bureau at 1-866-248-3049
or visit our website at www.simonspeakers.com.

Interior design by Alexis Minieri

Manufactured in the United States of America

10 9 8 7 6 5 4 3 2 1

Library of Congress Cataloging-in-Publication Data
Names: Perron, Cam, 1994– author. | Chiles, Nick, author.
Title: Comeback season : my unlikely story of friendship with the greatest living
   Negro League baseball players / by Cam Perron with Nick Chiles.
Description: First Gallery Books hardcover edition. | New York : Gallery Books, 2021.
Identifiers: LCCN 2020038081 (print) | LCCN 2020038082 (ebook) |
   ISBN 9781982153601 (hardback) | ISBN 9781982153618 (paperback) |
   ISBN 9781982153625 (ebook)
Subjects: LCSH: Negro leagues—History. | African American baseball players—
   Biography. | Discrimination in sports—United States—History. |
   Perron, Cam—Friends and associates.
Classification: LCC GV875.N35 P47 2021 (print) | LCC GV875.N35 (ebook) |
   DDC 796.35764089/96073—dc23
LC record available at https://lccn.loc.gov/2020038081
LC ebook record available at https://lccn.loc.gov/2020038082

ISBN 978-1-9821-5360-1
ISBN 978-1-9821-5362-5 (ebook)

To all former Negro League baseball players

Contents

Hank Aaron playing for the Indianapolis Clowns, 1952 (from a promotional postcard produced by the Clowns).

Foreword

by Henry "Hank" Aaron

Henry "Hank" Aaron was born in Mobile, Alabama, in 1934. In February 1952 he turned eighteen years old and joined the Indianapolis Clowns of the Negro Leagues. He played outstandingly for the Clowns, at one point leading the Negro American League in batting average, runs, hits, doubles, home runs, runs batted in, and total bases, and ranking third in stolen bases. He drew the notice of major-league scouts, and was signed in June 1952 to the Boston Braves' minor-league team the Eau Claire Bears. He rose quickly through the minors, and in 1954, he was called up to the major-league roster for the Braves. (The Braves had moved from Boston to Milwaukee in 1953, and would move again, to Atlanta, in 1966). Aaron played with the Braves for twenty seasons, from 1954 to 1974, and had one of the greatest major-league careers in history. He holds the record for being named to the most All-Star rosters (25); ranks first all time in runs batted in (2,297); first in total bases (6,856); second on the all-

time home runs list (755); won the World Series (1957); and was inducted into the Baseball Hall of Fame in his first year of eligibility (1982), having received votes on 97.8 percent of the ballots. He is currently senior vice president of the Atlanta Braves, and has worked in the Braves organization for nearly seventy years.

Let me start by saying if it hadn't been for the Indianapolis Clowns offering me a chance to play in the Negro Leagues, I don't know what would have happened to me. I have no idea what I would have done. They gave me the opportunity to keep playing a sport I wanted to play more than anything in the world.

My dad had played a little baseball, but he never went further than playing on a local team. My uncles also played a little on local teams. Up until I joined the Clowns in 1952, at age eighteen, I had only been playing on local teams as well. When the Clowns gave me the opportunity to show what I could do, I told myself: *Don't let this chance pass you by!*

When I was growing up in Mobile, Alabama, I taught myself how to hit by swinging at bottle caps with a broomstick. When you don't have a lot, you take it upon yourself to learn how to do things, to discover what you are capable of. But I never thought I was developing some kind of special talent by learning how to hit bottle caps. It's just what we had available. My friend Cornelius Giles, who is no longer with us, would pitch the bottle caps to me. Or I would toss them up myself. We would do this all day long.

FOREWORD

I've heard people say that the bottle caps gave me the eye to later hit a baseball so well, but I don't know if that's true. I feel like God was the one who gave me the eye to do some of the things in baseball I wound up doing. In addition to that, I took it upon myself to learn how to play the game the way it's supposed to be played. I told myself: *No matter what happens, you have to be the best you can possibly be.*

The first professional baseball game I saw was when the Clowns came to Mobile when I was fourteen, in 1948. They were playing against little scrap teams that were put together from players in Mobile. I was excited by what I saw on the field, but I also had an important realization that day. I knew I could play on the same level as those guys. I could compete on a professional level.

The atmosphere at that game was so much fun; the Black community was so excited. We had no other forms of entertainment—to us, this was baseball at its height. This was our major league. I saw kids on the field that day who easily could have put on a Major League Baseball uniform and played in the white league—though I wasn't thinking about the white league at the time. [Jackie Robinson had debuted with the Brooklyn Dodgers only a year earlier.] I just enjoyed watching them play.

I was seventeen years old in November 1951 when I heard from the Clowns that they wanted me to play with them the next year, after I turned eighteen in February. They sent me a contract for $200 a month. I thought I was in a dream. I couldn't believe I would get an opportunity to play in the

Negro Leagues—and they would actually pay me. It was the greatest thing that had ever happened to me. Two hundred dollars seemed like an awful lot of money—I felt like I was robbing the bank. I had certainly never seen that much money. When I was growing up in Mobile, a nickel was a lot of money to me. But to be honest, I would have played in the Negro Leagues for free; I just wanted to play baseball.

When I left Mobile and showed up to spring training in Winston-Salem, North Carolina, I didn't know whether I would even make the team and get a uniform. It was a lot colder in North Carolina and I didn't even have a jacket or warm clothes. All I was thinking was that I had to show them I could play.

When I walked out on the field for my first game wearing a Clowns uniform, I felt like I was something special. I was getting a chance to do the thing I had been wanting to do my entire life. I still wasn't thinking about the major league, about playing in the white leagues. I was just thinking about showing that I was capable of playing in the Negro Leagues, against that level of competition. If somebody had told me at the time that this was the highest I would ever go in baseball, I would have been fine with that. After all, we had no other choice at the time but to think that this was the highest we would go, and that we just had to do the best we could. We didn't know whether we would have the opportunity to play in the major league.

I was lucky; they discovered that I could really hit the ball. God had put His hands on me. He had showed me the direction. I was so happy—I had $2 a day for meal money; I could wash my clothes every day, which was something I appreciated since I didn't have anything else to put on. God showed me the way. I continued to have success.

Many years after my playing career was over and I had become an executive for the Braves, I heard that Major League Baseball was going to provide a pension to former Negro Leaguers, and I thought it was one of the greatest things that ever happened to the Negro Leagues. I was pleased that Major League Baseball was going to make sure things were made right. I didn't have anything to do with it, but I was very happy when they passed it.

I was impressed when I learned of the work that Cam Perron is doing on behalf of former Negro League players, getting them what they deserve. I know how very, very important his work has been to them. They didn't make much money when they were playing. Having an opportunity to receive a pension was one of the greatest things that could happen to them. There's no question Cam should be applauded. For too many of the players, there was nothing there for them before.

Negro League baseball has been so important to my life. I won't ever forget the way I felt when I walked on the field for the Clowns—like I was already in the major league. There was nothing else I wanted to be doing. And the Negro Leagues gave me the opportunity to go on to play Major League Baseball. Those months I spent on the Clowns helped me tremendously—not only teaching me how to play the game itself but also showing me that I belonged at that level. I'll never forget that.

Henry Aaron
Atlanta, Georgia
August 2020

Prologue

I had already filled my suitcase with baseballs, printed photographs, and multiple cameras before realizing that I'd forgotten to pack a change of clothes. I decided I could go without them. I'd only be staying in Alabama for one night. The autographs were more important.

The next morning, before the sun was fully up, I left my apartment just off the campus of Tulane University in New Orleans, and took a taxi to the train station. It was Friday, August 28, 2015. I had just arrived at Tulane the previous Sunday for the start of my junior year of college. Thankfully, my professors had understood when I explained why I needed to skip my Friday classes. I had to be in Birmingham for the opening of the Negro Southern League Museum—just the second museum in the entire country devoted to Negro League baseball, after the one in Kansas City. It was an event that I wouldn't have missed for the world. For me and a few of my closest friends, it was the culmination of years of work.

1

I found my Amtrak train at the station, and settled in for my first-ever journey by rail that wasn't on a crammed Boston subway car. The ride was scheduled to be seven hours and fifteen minutes. I wanted to get to Birmingham as quickly as possible, but there weren't any direct flights, and this had been the best option. I'd been buzzing with nervous excitement all week; the feeling was still there. I hooked up to the Wi-Fi; put on an eclectic playlist of Marvin Gaye, Funkadelic, Fleetwood Mac, and Soundgarden; and tried to relax.

Birmingham had become a second home to me of sorts over the previous six years. It was the place I'd been to most outside of Boston, where I grew up, and New Orleans, where I was now in school. Every year since 2010, I had joined a group of around fifty former Negro League players in downtown Birmingham for a weeklong reunion. These events had been put together by me and two men in their sixties, Dr. Layton Revel and Chef Clayton Sherrod, who I would be seeing in a matter of hours. We had chosen the city because of its rich history of Black professional baseball. It had the largest number of living former Negro League players of anywhere in the country, it was central to many other Southern cities where former players were still located, and it was also Chef Clayton's hometown.

Dr. Revel and Chef Clayton were the ones who had dreamed up the Negro Southern League Museum, and had been the primary engines of turning it into a reality. For years, they had pitched the idea to the city's political authorities, but hope came and went as fast as each mayor. Then, seem-

2

ingly all at once, the idea finally got traction. Budgeting and architectural designs were approved. I'd gone to the groundbreaking ceremony in May. And now, after only a matter of months, the ribbon cutting event was happening. An empty dirt field downtown, behind the home stadium of the Birmingham Barons—the Chicago White Sox AA minor-league affiliate team—had been selected as the site. Today, a fifteen-thousand-square-foot testament to the people who had participated in one of the least understood and most important sports leagues in American history would be officially opened. I could barely believe it.

As the train made its way through Mississippi, I thought of all of the letters and packages I had sent to former Negro League players who lived in that state. Odell Daniels of Byram; Russell Mosley of Shuqualak; Raymond Aguillard of Vossburg; and so many more. I'd never been to any of those towns, but I knew their area codes off the top of my head.

When 769 popped up on my phone, that was Daniels. He either wanted to catch up and chat, or would ask me to make him more baseball cards, which he could sign and give away to friends and family.

If the phone said 662, that was Mosley. I was still working on his pension, and he would most likely be checking in with me about it. I needed to find a newspaper article proving that he'd played for a fourth year in the Negro Leagues, in order for Major League Baseball to accept his pension application and approve his payout. I'd been digging through archives for years with no luck, but I'd tell him I was nowhere close to giving up.

3

If the number was 601, that was Aguillard. He would ask what I was up to, what project I had up my sleeve this time, and then would tell me about the latest happenings on his farm, where he had dogs, chickens, and a variety of other animals, including peacocks.

As the train passed through Picayune, Mississippi, a disaster occurred for a millennial like me—the Wi-Fi gave out, and with it, my music. This trip was going to last an eternity. How was I going to entertain myself? I pulled my suitcase down from the baggage hold and unzipped it to see what I could find.

The baseballs and photographs filling up my bag were all clean and unmarked: I'd brought them to be autographed. No matter how much my relationship to sports and fame had changed over the years, no matter how many players I'd met and befriended, one thing that I could never seem to put aside was my obsession with autograph collecting. I had been a collector as far back as I could remember; it was in my blood, and I didn't care to pretend otherwise. Signed baseballs, photographs, and trading cards filled the closets, dressers, and drawers of my room in my parents' house back in Boston. I wasn't interested in a ball signed by Mickey Mantle, which would be one of thousands. I was interested in a ball signed by Russell Mosley, who had not signed one since the late 1950s. For me, it wasn't about trophy hunting. It was about preserving history.

It had long been my goal to obtain a signed baseball from every former Negro League player that I interviewed and spoke with. Blue ink, ideally, right in the "sweet spot," at the narrowest point between the seams. If I really got my wish, I'd also ask them to write the names of the teams and the years they'd played above the signature; then their position or nickname below. An autographed baseball might seem like an unimportant thing, but to me it was an encapsulation of a career, long since passed but still remembered. As it turned out, these baseballs I so diligently collected had a destiny. Over the past few months, I'd sent many of them ahead of me to Birmingham. Dr. Revel had spent much of the summer driving truckloads of Negro League memorabilia from his home in Texas to Birmingham. From what he told me, the balls I'd sent were now encased on a wall in the museum, along with hundreds upon hundreds of others. I couldn't wait to see them again.

The train was delayed for more than an hour, and it was nearly 3:30 p.m. when it finally pulled into Birmingham. The ribbon cutting ceremony was scheduled to start at four, so my anxiety was hitting overdrive. I ran out of the station, jumped into a cab, with my suitcase in one hand and a camera in the other, and went straight to the museum. Fortunately it was only a half-mile drive and I was there in no time. Chef Clayton Sherrod was waiting for me. "Cam, you made it," he said, as he helped me out of the cab. Then he took a hard look at me and asked, "Have you eaten?" It wasn't a surprising question, given that he is indeed an elite chef, but I realized that he was actually right—I had been so focused on getting to Birmingham for the past nine hours that I hadn't eaten all day. "I'll get something soon, don't worry," I told him.

I found a spot to stash my suitcase, and took stock of the crowd. There were about twenty former ballplayers, along with family members, city officials, and members of the wider community, gathered around. I knew most of them well. The annual reunion had become such a popular event in Birmingham that it seemed like we'd all gotten to know everyone in town. Some of the players had put on replica jerseys for the teams they had once played for; others wore suits and top hats. I was used to the wheelchairs and walkers. One of the players, Roosevelt Jackson, was not only ninety-seven years old but also blind.

The ribbon cutting ceremony for the Birmingham Negro Southern League Museum, August 28, 2015. *Front row, from left:* Roosevelt Jackson, Mayor William A. Bell, Oliver "Son" Ferguson, and Merritt "Pee Wee" Stoves.

Within a matter of minutes, the mayor of Birmingham, William A. Bell, joined all of the players congregated in front of the brand-new, two-story glass-and-brick building. I stepped back to take on my unofficial but well-established role of event photographer for our group. Scissors were passed around and a long ribbon was spread out. Cuts were made, the ribbon fell, and cheers rang out. I captured the moment.

I grabbed a sandwich and joined the players and guests, hugging, smiling, seeing how everyone was doing. Then the museum doors opened, and we all went inside. One of the first things I saw was the "wall of balls." The display case ran the length of the entire entrance hallway. There were signed balls from floor to ceiling, alphabetically arranged by last name. I walked along the wall, spotting many of the balls I'd sent. They called to mind the stories, experiences, and histories I'd come to know so well. Players I'd spent countless hours with and grown close to had died over the past few years. I knew it wouldn't be long before there weren't any more Negro League players left. But this place, and these balls, would be here. As I took in the museum over the next hour with Dr. Revel, Chef Clayton, and the players, laughing, remembering, teasing, debating, like we always did, I kept coming back to the baseballs. Each time I did, I couldn't help but smile, just to know they were there.

There were a couple of local reporters at the ribbon cutting ceremony, and before I headed to the La Quinta hotel where I'd booked a room, one approached me. He had noticed and been a little bit confused about why all of these seventy-, eighty-, and ninety-year-old Black men were treating me like something between a grandson and a pal. So we started talking, and it wasn't long before I got a version of the same question I'd been hearing for nearly a decade.

"How does a white kid from a suburb of Boston become friends with all of these former Negro League baseball players?"

CHAPTER 1

The Collector

Before I'd ever heard of the Negro Leagues, before I bonded with hundreds of aging former baseball players who became some of my best friends, before I had my life changed by living avatars of American history, I was a curious kid growing up just outside of Boston, fascinated by anything that I considered old.

My hometown of Arlington, Massachusetts, sits right next to Cambridge, where Harvard and MIT are located. The houses and average incomes have since gotten bigger, but when I was growing up in the late 1990s and early 2000s it was a solidly middle-class place of about forty-three thousand people. It was also overwhelmingly white—a whopping 90 percent, according to the 2000 census. Only 1.7 percent of the town's population was Black.

I wasn't really conscious of it at the time, but from a young age, I sensed that as a white kid in middle-class America, there were rules, expectations, and parameters I was meant to follow. I was determined to make my own choices, do things my own way, and I was lucky to have parents who supported me. So, at each step, if my peers went right, I went left.

My mother, Lauren, says I came out of the womb in 1994 with an unusual interest in older people. She worked as a shoe designer for the company Stride Rite, and there was a daycare facility at her office, so she brought me into work with her every day, from the time I was eight weeks old up until I was four. I don't remember much from that time, but apparently I would ask my mom for the names of the parents of the other children who were in the daycare, then repeat the names to myself to memorize them. When the parents would come in to drop off or pick up their kids, I'd say hello to each one of them, by name. "It was the funniest thing," my mom says. "Cam always appreciated what adults did. He was the kind of kid that if we had people over and they brought their kids, when the kids were running around or doing something, Cam wanted to be with the grown-ups, hearing what they had to say."

My father, Dan, speculated that this precocious habit might lead me to a career in politics. But looking back, this was really about me liking the feeling of being taken seriously by adults, and a politician isn't exactly the model of a person who people take seriously anymore. (I'm not trying to be funny here; just telling the truth.)

I realized early on that my interest in adults wasn't shared by my peers. I wasn't a loner by any means—I had friends and I enjoyed spending time with them—but the kids I grew

My dad, Dan, my mom, Lauren, and me at age twelve.

up with seemed to believe the world revolved around them. I struggled with the way they spent their time. I wondered: *Did we have to play Mario Kart whenever we got together, for hours on end? Was junk food, like Lay's chips, pretzels, cookies, the only option?* That all may sound like a kid's dream, but my mind didn't work that way. I would get back to my room after one of those afternoons, sit on my bed, and ask myself what the hell I had accomplished all day. I guess you could say I was an old soul. I was already searching for personal fulfillment, and I thought that older people might just hold the answers.

This might also explain why I was so fascinated by history. When I was five years old I became captivated by a perfume

11

bottle that had been owned by my great-grandmother. My mom says I would ask endless questions about the bottle—where it came from, who had made it—and soon, I became interested in all kinds of old stuff.

My grandfather Joe—my father's father—was a longtime coin collector, and when I was nine years old, he helped me start a collection of my own. He took me with him to an enormous outdoor fair called the Brimfield Antique Show and Flea Market that was about a half hour from his house in Dudley, Massachusetts. Brimfield is the largest outdoor antique market in America. It's held three times a year, and is made up of thousands of vendors stretching for more than a mile, who sell just about anything that could conceivably be called antique—guns, furniture, toys, *Playboy* magazines, you name it. More than a million visitors typically go to Brimfield each year. My eyes practically popped out of their sockets when I saw it for the first time.

As I walked around the fair with my grandfather, I was fascinated by the idea that every item had a history of some kind. I imagined being able to touch something and instantly know its story, its meaning, its lifetime of lessons. How cool would that be?

Since my grandfather's focus was on coins, we spent most of our time visiting coin vendors, and I was quickly hooked. Now, *these* were objects with stories behind them, I realized. One of the first items I bought was an 1856 Braided Hair Half Cent. As its name suggests, it was originally worth half a penny. The tiny coin was in poor condition, no longer in circulation, and had little monetary value to collectors—which is why I was able to buy it for $2—but I was enthralled to own something that old, with so much history behind it. It was the start of my coin collection, and a number of early lessons about the ins and outs of collecting.

I loved learning about the history of the 1856 Braided Hair Half Cent, but I also wanted to understand why that coin wasn't valuable and others were, so I dove into research on the prices of different coins. One of the first things I discovered was that pre-1965 quarters and dimes were more valuable than post-1965 versions because they contained silver. That piece of information sent me on a hunt through all the old change my dad had stashed in various places around the house. My mission was to unearth the old coins with hidden silver and rescue them from a future trip to the Coinstar machine at the local supermarket. I was turning into a nine-year-old silver prospector, and learning along the way about the importance of the quality of the materials that went into making collectible items.

When I was nine, my dad also showed me a bunch of Bicentennial quarters he had collected from 1976. Surely these special edition coins would have gained value all these years later? But as I found out, the bicentennial coin was *still* only worth 25 cents. I learned that so many people had saved them, thinking they would someday be sought after, that the mass hoarding had created the opposite of the intended effect: an oversupply, and no demand. This was my introduction to the crucial connection between rarity and value.

My grandparents bought me coin books that I could use to carefully organize my growing collection. A big thing at the time was collecting all fifty of the state quarters, which were being issued with unique, state-specific designs. The government issued a new state every few months. I lost interest when I saw how easy it was to get all fifty—if you didn't want to wait to come by them on your own merits, you could just purchase the ones you were missing for 75 cents each. This was disappointing, because the hunt had already become as important as the find to me, and I thought that the hunt should be difficult. If you could skip the hard part, there was no fun or challenge in it. Another lesson about collecting learned.

So it was the old, valuable, rare, and hard-to-find coins that my grandfather and I liked best. Those items were worth more, yes—but they also had the most interesting histories. When I held a coin from 1943 in my hand, I could imagine a kid clutching it in his palm as he picked out a gumball at the corner store during World War II. An item like that made history feel alive to me.

When I discovered that there was a collectible store in the nearby town of Lexington, I begged my mother to bring me there whenever possible. Lexington Coin looked like a house from the outside, but inside there were glass cases filled with coins from all over the world, as well as stamps and old paper currency. There were also large buckets of miscellaneous unsorted foreign coins for $0.10 a piece. I'd walk in with $4 or $5 burning a hole in my pocket, browse the display cases of ancient gold and silver coins, and ask the owner questions. He'd answer seriously, speaking to me like a collector instead of an elementary school kid. To be treated that way by an adult made me love my trips there all the more. I gravitated toward the $0.10 buckets, as they fit my budget and filled my mind with possibilities of scoring a rare find. I picked up foreign coins, some of them hundreds of years old, from nations like Palestine and Yugoslavia, expanding my sense of history. Unfortunately, the ones I got weren't valuable, but they were still unusual, historical, and therefore, in my mind, cool.

I soon added comic book collecting to my interests. It was easier to pursue the hobby on my own because we had two comic book stores right in Arlington. Magic Dragon Comics in Arlington Center was a dimly lit, studio apartment–sized store that looked like it could cave in at any moment. The hours posted online and displayed on the window were never followed; the owner seemed to open and close the store whenever he felt like it. I got the sense that he sometimes slept in the back. You could barely walk in the place—it was arranged more like a yard sale than a typical store—but in the large boxes with dozens of comic books for 50 cents each or four-for-a-dollar, it seemed like there was potential for a score. The other store, Comicazi, was in Arlington Heights and it was much larger. The walls and shelves were filled with thousands of action figures, small toys, and hundreds of higher-end vintage and new comic books. In the back, there were thousands of comics sorted alphabetically by title, and each was individually priced.

I never even cracked open the comics I bought—they were entirely about the hunt, the history, the value, and the collecting habit for me, not about the content. I would spend hours in the stores, rifling through the cheap bins, looking for comics that my research told me might be worth more than their face value, and picking up little bits of information as I went. I learned that you could tell the age of the book by the cover price; a dime meant it was from the 1940s or early 1950s. I found out early edition Amazing Spider-Man and Hulk comics were worth huge amounts of money. A mint issue *Spider-Man* #1 would likely be worth more than $10,000. I even purchased a few of the most affordable Spider-Man and Hulk comics with the earliest dates I could find, settling on *Amazing Spider-Man* #60 and *The Incredible Hulk* #151. I decided to keep the Spider-Man I'd bought, but I aimed to test the waters with the Hulk comic to see if there was anyone out there who might pay me good money for it. This led me to my first foray into the wide world of selling collectibles on the internet.

I looked into opening an eBay account, but they didn't allow second graders to do that, so I convinced my mom to open an account in her name that I could use. I then created a seven-day auction where I listed the comic with a starting bid of $0.99. I was beyond ecstatic when I got a hit, but it turned out it was for the minimum amount. It would be the only bid I'd get. After I went through the bother of packing up the Hulk comic and shipping it out, I wound up paying a whole lot more than the 99 cents the buyer had paid me. It was a failed entrepreneurial venture. Only weeks later did I find out the buyer was one of my dad's coworkers. Dad, who is an accountant, had gotten such a kick out of me listing items on eBay that he'd talked about it in his office, and one of his colleagues had bought my comic.

While the focus of my collections shifted over the course of my elementary school years, from coins, to comic books, to baseball cards, and beyond, one thing remained: my obsession with the band Nirvana. It had started when I was five years old. My twin brothers Ryan and Jack had just been born, and I didn't want to listen to their baby music in the car—I wanted to listen to the rock music that my mom liked. So when our cassette player broke with Nirvana's *Nevermind* album stuck inside, I was thrilled. We were forced to play it over and over again, and soon, they were my favorite band. I wanted to know everything about them and their lead singer, Kurt Cobain.

When my friends started listening to the boy bands of the time, like NSYNC, I, as usual, went the other way, and stuck with Nirvana. I couldn't let my preoccupation with them stop at listening to the music, either; I had to go all in, and start a collection. On eBay, I found Nirvana fans selling all sorts of rare foreign-label bootleg CDs and imports, like a live recording from a show the group did in Europe. I would bid and even win sometimes. In the third grade, I used all my birthday money to buy an unreleased Nirvana recording.

I also joined forums like the Nirvana Yahoo Fan Group to research the band and get to know other devotees of the group. In the fourth grade, I made my own Nirvana website—a fan

17

page where I posted pictures of the rare CDs and other items I had collected. I taught myself basic HTML coding, designed the website, and had it hosted on a free platform. I used a basic template and incorporated the coding to add in the photographs. Back then, it would take forever to properly code one photograph; you couldn't just pop it in and call it a day. I didn't know it at the time, but these skills I was learning—how to use the internet to connect with people, and find things that others couldn't—would be critical to my future as a Negro League researcher.

At the end of fifth grade, my interest in Nirvana helped teach me one more lesson: that even adults could be misguided, and through prejudice or ignorance, they could fail to see the merits of something that was important and deserved attention. I had to pick a historical figure, write a research paper, and present it in front of the class. Of course, I chose Kurt Cobain. My teacher, Mrs. Foley, was not excited at all about the idea of me presenting the class with a report glorifying someone who had taken his own life. In fact, her first reaction to my idea was a decisive "No." I realized that many adults had a negative view of the guy, which was likely due to their understanding about him being limited to knowing about his drug addiction and death by suicide.

I was reminded of a time the year before, when none of my classmates' parents would let them buy 50 Cent's *Get Rich or Die Tryin'* CD. The reason they cited was that the record had a parental advisory label, meaning it was inappropriate for kids—and that may have been true. I suspected that the fact that it was rap music had something to do with it, too, and I wasn't having it. So I burned copies of the album myself, on blank CDs, and sold them for $10—or traded them for base-ball cards.

I begged Mrs. Foley to let me do the report on Cobain, telling her I would make a strong case that he was an im-portant figure in music who shouldn't be judged solely by how his life ended. My mother also weighed in, meeting with Mrs. Foley to help me make my case. Finally, my teacher re-lented. I knew the pressure was on; she was going to be pay-ing closer attention to my presentation than to the kids who picked the obvious choices, like Martin Luther King Jr. or the Wright Brothers.

When I got an A on the paper and presentation, I felt I had achieved a big victory. I had taken a chance and refused to back down after getting an initial rejection. It was an impor-tant moment for me, giving me confidence that my view of the world and my interests, unusual as they may have been, had merit.

The Cobain project was the culmination of the first phase of my collecting habit, and brought together all of the things I'd learned. I loved history, I was a good researcher, I valued things that were rare, and if other people didn't understand my interests—so be it.

CHAPTER 2

Finding My Way into Sports

When I was about eight, I started getting involved in organized team sports, and taking them more seriously. At first, I tried everything—soccer, lacrosse, hockey, baseball—my schedule was jam-packed with sports, as it is for many kids in suburban America. Hockey and baseball were the two I gravitated toward over time. I wasn't the worst athlete, but I was far from the best, so I came up with a plan for hockey that would ensure I'd get plenty of playing time: I volunteered to be goalie. Having pucks fired at your head wasn't something most kids were eager to do, meaning I didn't have a whole lot of competition for the position. It became my own little thing that nobody could take away from me.

The first few years we played at a rink about a mile and a half from my house. I had a good time with my friends. I even enjoyed going to practice. But then the coaches began pushing us to sign up for the Arlington travel league, in addition to the local league. Between the two leagues I was playing upward of seventy-five games per season. Where I'd previously played a game down the road and then come home to have the rest of the day to myself, now I had 5 a.m. games in Wilmington, Massachusetts, which was thirty minutes away. My dad and I would have to leave so early that the Dunkin' Donuts wasn't open yet. We'd be so tired on those drives that we would blast rock albums in the car to help us wake up. We always selected the CDs the night before (a favorite of ours was Pearl Jam's debut album, *Ten*).

After the painfully early Saturday-morning game was over, I'd usually have to go back to Arlington to play in another game at 3 p.m. with my local team. The coaches were over-the-top with the intensity. One acted like his son was on the verge of going pro. Even at the time, I thought: *We're in sixth grade, nobody is going pro.* It wasn't fun anymore; the whole ordeal became a chore for me. It was disturbing how the intensity of the adults controlling my town's youth sports leagues drained the joy out of it.

At the end of that tiring hockey season, I said, "You know what? I quit." I think my parents were relieved. My mother would come across other mothers in town and they would ask, "Oh my God, why did Cam quit hockey? Is everything okay?"

"He just wasn't into it anymore," she'd say. "It wasn't fun, so he said he's done."

"I can't believe that," they'd say.

It didn't even cross their minds that having a kid play seventy-five games in a season was overkill. It was one of the first times where I realized, *If I don't have to do something I don't like, why do it?*

I did continue to play organized baseball for many years, though, which was still fun for me, even if I wasn't playing every inning or dreaming of going pro.

As unremarkable as my own sports career was, playing on teams, baseball in particular, led me to be a sports fan, and the one thing I shared with every boy in New England in the early 2000s was a love for the Boston Red Sox. Not only was the team winning games, but they were doing it in colorful ways. I first started really caring about the team in 2001, and followed their daily dramas like a soap opera fan. Star outfielder Johnny Damon and first baseman/outfielder Kevin Millar nicknamed the team "the Idiots" because of their cavalier attitude toward the eighty-six years that had passed without the Sox winning a championship, and the "Curse of the Bambino."

It's hard to overemphasize how much everybody in the Boston area became obsessed by the Red Sox in 2004, as they marched through the regular season into the postseason. We were desperate for this team to be the one to break the curse. I knew every detail about each player on the team, even the utility players on the bench. Like everybody else in the area, I went nuts when the Sox won the 2004 World Series, sweeping the St. Louis Cardinals after accomplishing the mind-boggling feat of coming back from a three-games-to-zero deficit to beat the Yankees in the American League Championship Series. There is probably no creature on the planet happier than a ten-year-old boy whose favorite sports team wins the championship.

Around this time, my interest in the Sox and my interest in collecting coincided. At the first Red Sox game I went to, I met Cesar Crespo, who was a reserve infielder. I was so psyched when he signed my hat. Crespo never played that night, but it was still exciting to me to get this memento from a player in real time. It was the start of what would quickly become my collecting focus: sports memorabilia and baseball cards. In 2005, following the World Series win, every business in the area was trying to get a little piece of the Sox magic. McDonald's issued a Red Sox trading card set, which was inserted for several weeks into the Sunday issue of the *Boston Globe*. The *Globe* also teamed up with local convenience stores, including Walgreens, to sell collectible pins for each player on the team. Dunkin' Donuts gave away cups featuring Red Sox stars at their local shops. The town was on fire with that stuff. And I couldn't sit still until I had every piece. The players, not wanting to miss out on this prime chance for extra cash, began doing more promotional events. Getting Johnny Damon or David Ortiz to make an appearance at your business could garner a great deal of attention. I began scanning the newspaper, looking for meet-and-greet appearances that I could attend. When I saw that Johnny Damon was doing a signing at a nearby Borders bookstore for his new book, *Idiot: Beating "The Curse" and Enjoying the Game of Life*, I begged my mother to bring me.

"Mom, we have to go!" I told her. "We have to go!"

My mom liked him, too, so it wasn't that hard to convince her. I felt like it was my destiny to meet Johnny. He and I shared the same birthday, November 5, and we're both lefties.

My mom took me, my brothers Jack and Ryan, and two of my friends to the signing, and when we got there, we found a crowd of at least five hundred people already waiting. It was also snowing outside. But we braved the weather and joined the back of the line. Everyone kept going into the Starbucks to get snacks and warm up, but I refused to leave the line.

We had finally made it inside the store after waiting for about three hours, when a woman came up to us and said, "I'm sorry, we're going to have to cut you off."

"Excuse me?" my mom asked.

"Johnny is going to have to go home. There won't be time for you to get his autograph."

I couldn't let it go down like that, not without putting up a fight.

"I'm not leaving the line!" I said.

The people around us were just as upset as we were. After a bit of grumbling, we started chanting, "Don't leave, Johnny! Don't leave, Johnny!" As others heard it, they joined in until the chant reverberated through the bookstore. We could see Johnny look up from the table where he was signing books and start laughing. He announced that he would stay until every book got signed. It wound up taking him eight and a half hours.

When we finally got to the front of the line, Johnny was

the nicest guy. I took a picture with him, and he let me try on his World Series ring. I excitedly told him we shared a birthday, and he smiled. But when I started talking to him about music, he glanced at me with real curiosity. I had been reading through his book while we waited, and I'd been really interested in the section where he talked about his favorite groups. He'd written that one of the perks of being a ballplayer he liked most was getting to meet and jump onstage with acts like Godsmack and Creed, both of whom I was a fan of as well. I'd wanted to stand out from the rest of the people he'd met that day, so that he would remember me, and I could tell that I'd achieved my goal. He held up the line and actually chatted with me for a few minutes.

Me with Red Sox star Johnny Damon in April 2005 at Borders bookstore in Braintree, Massachusetts.

As we were walking out, my mother said, "It seemed like he was genuinely interested in you, Cam." I'm guessing I was the first person to talk about music with him that day. Later that year, I saw Johnny at a rock concert at the Avalon in Boston, doing exactly what he'd said he loved: jumping onstage for a rendition of the Red Sox fan-favorite song "Dirty Water," performed by his teammate Bronson Arroyo's band.

Over the next few months, my family continued taking me to Red Sox players' appearances. We went to see Kevin Millar at a local store, but we got there too late to meet him. We convinced a guy who worked at the store to go get his autograph on his baseball card for me before he left. We also braved another huge line and went to see Big Papi himself, David Ortiz, at a giant arcade called Good Time Emporium in Somerville. We waited about four hours to get to the front of the line. As we were about to meet Ortiz, somebody told us he wasn't going to sign any of the Red Sox gear we had brought with us.

"Huh?" I said.

"He's not signing anything."

They had advertised that Big Papi would take a picture with each attendee and sign one of their items. Now they were reneging. I was not happy, but it didn't look like the scene for a Damon-like insurrection. I tucked my Ortiz baseball card back in my pocket. They wound up handing out pre-signed eight-by-eleven photos of Ortiz. Even worse, they had us gather with twenty other people we didn't know to take a group photo with Ortiz—then they tried to charge us $25 for the privilege. My mom and I looked at each other, thinking *What the hell?* It was thoroughly ridiculous.

I had loved watching these guys on the field, especially during their magical run to the championship, but I was getting turned off by the crass commercialism of these interactions. My family didn't go to a lot of games—my parents had their hands full with me and my younger brothers, and ticket prices became exorbitant after 2004—but whenever we did go, I would notice the same patterns at the sites where fans gathered to get autographs at the game. The big stars would ignore us while the benchwarmers would come over to sign. I was open to having a different relationship with professional sports; I just didn't know yet what that would be.

Baseball cards were becoming my main collecting focus as I entered middle school. Whenever we went to the gas station or Walgreens, where packs of Topps baseball cards were for sale by the checkout counter, I would be elated. There were eight to ten cards in each $2 pack. I started to apply the skills I'd learned from my coin, comic book, and Nirvana collections. I'd keep an eye out in particular for cards labeled as "game-used," meaning Topps included something like a piece of a player's actual bat used in a game. The card would be numbered like an art print, telling you this was the eighteenth out of one hundred that had been made. I felt like I'd won the lottery when I opened a pack and saw that a tiny piece of a bat David Ortiz had broken in a game was affixed to one of my cards.

I started making trips to a small baseball card store in Cambridge called the Card Dog. It was next to an appliance store in a building a couple blocks from Cambridge's Fresh Pond strip malls. If you blinked, you'd miss it. The store had glass display cases with higher-end cards in them, and back shelves behind the counter with various unopened packs of cards. On the other side of the store were hundreds of cardboard boxes with unsorted baseball cards, stacked all the way to the water-damaged ceiling.

I'd wander in and sift through the boxes, looking for interesting cards I could afford. The newest game-used cards could be worth as much as $100 on eBay, and I made some money off of finding and then quickly selling a few of those. But a month or two later, the price would have dropped to $40 or less, showing me that these cards didn't retain their value after the hype wore off. I realized that if I wanted to find items that were really worth something, I'd have to start looking back in time, just as I'd done with coins and comic books.

Peter, the owner of the Card Dog, got familiar with me over the course of my repeat visits, and saw that I was trying to be a serious collector.

"You want to see the old stuff?" he asked me one day.

He went in the back and pulled out a box that contained cards that went all the way back to the 1940s and '50s. They were in terrible shape, beat up almost beyond recognition, so I knew they wouldn't be worth much. Still, I was intrigued by the histories of the players they featured.

I started thinking up ways I could make more money to

feed my collecting habit. I would go around the neighborhood after a big snowstorm and ask people if I could shovel for them. I made as much as $150 in a day that way. This opportunity was only available to me after a winter storm, though, so when spring came, I started making money by umpiring baseball games in the kiddie league.

I found out that there was a memorabilia auction that took place in Arlington on a Friday night once a month, where hundreds of collectible sports items would be for sale. I began to skip out on get-togethers at the skating rink with my middle school friends to attend the auctions instead. That's when this hobby kicked into the next gear, and started to become an obsession.

The auction company was called Hall's Nostalgia, and it had an impressive history. In the early 1960s, it had started as one of the first baseball card stores in America, as well as one of the first sports memorabilia auction companies. The monthly card and memorabilia auction that Hall's Nostalgia ran was held at a Knights of Columbus hall and attended by roughly one hundred people—almost all of them men over the age of fifty. I would get there at 5 p.m. along with the other collectors, for the auction preview. The event organizers would lay out a spread of cold cuts, soda, and chips, and for two hours we would look through the various lots, taking notes, and cross-checking them with the auction catalog, which described all of the items for sale that evening. After I became a regular, Hall's Nostalgia put me on their mailing list and started sending me the auction catalog in advance, giving me more time to evaluate the items, mark up which ones were interesting to me, and preplan my maximum bids. I made two new friends at the auctions: Ryan, an artist in his early thirties who was the second-youngest attendee, and Bob, a retiree in his early sixties. I'd sit between the two of them during the proceedings, and they'd whisper little tidbits of information to me. "Cam, that card is trimmed, stay away from that," Ryan would say, educating me about a shady practice in which vintage cards would be slightly trimmed in order to make them appear to be in better condition.

In the process, I was learning all about the history of baseball cards, diving deep into what I was coming to see was an area rich with stories and unbelievable characters.

I found out that baseball cards—and trading cards in general—were thought up by tobacco company executives in the 1880s, led by James "Buck" Duke, who realized that the companies could promote cigarette smoking by inserting cards in their cigarette boxes. Initially, the cards featured popular actresses, like Madame Rhéa from France. Duke even had employees go to the immigration waypoints in New York and hand out free cigarettes with the trading cards of actresses inside the packs to newly arriving immigrants, aiming to turn them into loyal smokers.

By the late 1800s, Buck Duke's company was putting all sorts of different types of cards in the packs, including those featuring athletes. Incredibly, one goal was to entice children to buy cigarettes, because they'd want to collect complete sets of cards. Duke even produced loose-leaf portfolio books to make it easy for children to collect and organize their sets. But the gimmick proved *too* successful—the cards became so popular and expensive to produce that they started to eat away at the tobacco companies' profits. In 1889, the powerful Duke convinced the heads of the five largest tobacco companies to form a monopoly, called the American Tobacco Company. One major advantage of coming together: they could stop printing the expensive card sets, because they would no longer have to worry about keeping an edge over competitors.

After the monopoly was formed, sports cards effectively disappeared for the next two decades. But they returned with a bang in 1909 when the American Tobacco Company produced a baseball card now known as the T206 Honus Wagner, still considered the most prized card in the collecting world. There are estimated to be fewer than one hundred T206 Wagners in existence. The rarity, lore, and the competitiveness of collectors have driven up the price of these cards, and they now sell for several million dollars.

Over time, baseball cards began to be produced by companies like Topps that were not connected to the tobacco industry, and by the 1980s and '90s, there were several hundred companies manufacturing competing card sets. It became impossible for children to keep up with the dizzying number of cards on the market. An estimated 81 billion cards were produced each year during this time—more than three hundred cards for every American, every year. In the eyes of many, this turned what had been an innocent American childhood pastime through the mid-twentieth century into a cutthroat business filled with multimillionaire investors. A lot of young people lost interest—leaving just the adults looking to use baseball cards to hit it rich.

The market hit its peak in 1991, when the sales of cards reached $1.2 billion. But the baseball card market crashed in August 1994, when major-league players went on strike. The players' strike generated so much anger at the sport that Americans simply stopped buying baseball cards for a while. The industry has since recovered to an impressive degree, though, in large part thanks to the democratizing power of the internet, which has brought younger people back into the fun of card collecting.

By the time I was in middle school, another unstoppable force had already been making its impact felt on card collecting: video games. While I was at the Hall's Nostalgia auctions—the rare kid in a world populated by adults—most of my friends were spending their free time playing Xbox.

There were *some* other kids who shared my interest in baseball cards and sports memorabilia, however, to be sure. And a chance encounter that I had around this time with Chris, an acquaintance my own age, opened my eyes to a whole new world. Chris probably has no idea what he did for me; he might not even remember my name. But one day, I found myself at his house. We were talking about baseball memorabilia, and he said, "Let me show you something." He left the room and came back with a stack of cards. He explained to me that he and his father wrote letters to former baseball players and would get signed cards back from them in the mail. My mind was blown. This was far cooler than standing in line for hours on end to be ignored by a current Red Sox player, or combing through a dusty old box at the Card Dog looking for vintage cards that were about to disintegrate. This was actual, personal contact with players. It was connection. It was history. Chris and his dad were effectively pen pals with former major leaguers.

Chris told me about a website called SportsCollectors.Net, where you could find a trove of information about athletes: their mailing addresses; how long it typically took them to respond to letters, if they responded at all; whether they charged a fee. I spent hours on the site, fascinated and thrilled. I saw that two hundred people had written to Alex Rodriguez and no one had gotten a response. On the other hand, every person who wrote to Duke Snider, a star of the Dodgers in the 1940s and '50s, had gotten a response within a week. I came up with a plan: go to the baseball card store and buy specific cards featuring older players, then send the players the cards in the mail requesting an autograph. A new obsession was born.

I even developed a form letter:

Hi, my name is Cam. I'm 12 years old. I'm a big baseball fan. I'm a catcher. I've been playing for the last four or five years. I've read a lot about you, even though you were much before my time. I've recently started collecting autographs of baseball legends, and I'd love if you could please autograph the enclosed baseball card. Thank you so much. Hope all is well.

I made sure to follow the tips I read on the site: send a self-addressed stamped envelope, and handwrite your letter, because it will increase your chances of getting a response. My hours at the baseball card store and the memorabilia shows were suddenly filled with purpose. I'd come up with a list containing several dozen promising names from the SportsCollectors site, then set out to find several cards for each guy on the list. I would typically then send them at least three to five cards to sign; I wanted duplicates so that I would have a supply to trade or sell. If I was ambitious, I might send them a baseball or two to sign as well, though that was a much more expensive proposition for me, because I had to buy the balls and they weren't cheap.

It didn't take long for me to realize that it wasn't worth my time to try to get autographs from current players, because they rarely complied or even responded. So I focused on a variety of former MLB Hall of Famers, retired All-Stars, and various average players, primarily from the 1940s to the 1970s. These included Lee MacPhail, Luis Tiant, Al Kaline, George Kell, Rollie Fingers, and Duke Snider.

By the beginning of seventh grade, I was sending out a minimum of forty letters a week to players. When Christmas came around, all I wanted were stamps, envelopes, and baseballs—the tools of my new trade. I literally waited by the mailbox every day at 6 p.m., heart racing, gazing down the street waiting for the little white mail truck to appear. I would have days when I would get a stack of as many as eight envelopes back in the mail from former players. If the mailman didn't come, I would be incensed—I figured it was nearly statistically impossible for me to go a day without getting anything back, given how many letters I was sending out. I found out that our mail carrier was the head of the local union and he sometimes worked half days—yeah, I got that deep into it. At least once every two weeks I'd call the post office and yell at somebody on the phone that the Perrons were being mistreated.

As my confidence and skill with this type of collecting grew, I started becoming fascinated by the challenge of the hunt. I saw on the SportsCollectors website that four or five hundred other people had been successful in getting autographs from players like Bobby Doerr and Sparky Anderson, and I began to want a higher degree of difficulty. (Incidentally, Bobby Doerr, the famed 1930s and '40s Boston Red Sox Hall of Famer, was one of the friendliest guys I reached out to; he always replied within a week.) That's when I discovered the "cup of coffee" players—so named because they had only been in the big leagues long enough to get a cup of coffee.

Players who only appeared in one game in the majors wouldn't have baseball cards, and wouldn't be easy to find. At this time, in 2007, internet research wasn't nearly as accessible or robust as it is today. Google was not yet seemingly all-knowing. I threw myself into the corners of the internet to find information on players who probably hadn't gotten an autograph request in years. This made it all the more thrilling for me when an envelope came back with their signature on the index card I had sent them. They would sometimes send along a note with the autograph, telling me how appreciative they were. That was way cooler to me than getting an autograph back from someone who treated it perfunctorily. It felt like my recognition of these little-known players meant something to them. Their recognition, in return, certainly meant something to me.

In the midst of all my internet research, I was stunned to discover that there was a "cup of coffee" player who lived in my own town, named Tom Yewcic. He had played in one game with the Detroit Tigers in June 1957. He played three innings as a catcher and he had one unsuccessful at bat. But then Yewcic went on to have a successful football career with the Boston Patriots in the 1960s before they became the New England Patriots. He played quarterback, wide receiver, running back, and punter. He still holds the team record for the longest run by a Patriots punter—twenty yards in a 1962 win over the Oakland Raiders. Yewcic and Tom Brady are the only Pats players who have punted, thrown a touchdown pass, caught a pass, and run for a touchdown.

Once I saw that he still lived in Arlington, I looked up his number and called him immediately. I told him I was a young baseball fan and collector. I asked if I could come over to interview him about his baseball career. He graciously agreed. I walked to his house since it was less than ten blocks away from mine. I had some baseballs and index cards for him to sign, plus a few pictures I had printed out of him in a Tigers uniform. We talked for more than an hour. I probably was one of the few people who asked him solely about his base-ball career—I didn't care much about football. I was more interested in making connections by throwing out names of baseball teammates who had played alongside him during his four seasons in the minor leagues. He signed all of my stuff and also signed a print for me of him in a Boston Patriots uniform.

I was also excited that year when I got a response in the mail from Red Borom, who was ninety-three years old at the time. He had played fifty-five games with the Detroit Tigers in 1945, including appearances in two games of the 1945 World Series, which the Tigers ultimately won. Borom's chief claim to fame was that he was the runner on third base when Hank Greenberg won the pennant for the Tigers by hitting a grand slam in the ninth inning of the final game of the season. In Borom's letter to me, he mentioned that spe-cifically, saying: "Yes, it was a real treat to have had Hank Greenberg as a teammate. I'm fortunate to have known him. In the final game of 1945 he hit a bases loaded home run in the ninth inning to win the pennant. I was the runner on 3rd base." Reading Borom's handwritten letter on lined paper in cursive, about this monumental moment in baseball history, was thrilling to me.

There was something much more special about these inter-actions I was starting to have than anything I'd experienced beforehand in my life as a collector. They were personal, meaningful, and with players who had been overlooked by others. I began to crave this sort of communication. And it was this desire that led me, by chance, circumstance, and instinct, to the Negro Leagues, where I would find what I was looking for in ways I never could have expected. It would come to alter the course of my life.

CHAPTER 3

Hello, Negro Leagues

When I was at Chris's house, after he introduced me to the SportsCollectors.Net site and showed me the letters that he and his dad had gotten back from players, he brought out an autographed baseball card that intrigued me. It was from Buck O'Neil; Chris and his dad had gotten it through the mail. Buck O'Neil had just passed away at the end of 2006, and something about the name and the card stuck in my mind. When I went home and looked him up, I saw that he had become a legendary coach for the Chicago Cubs after his playing and managing days with the Kansas City Monarchs were over. The Monarchs, I learned, were perhaps the best-known, most successful, and longest-running team in the Negro Leagues. In fact, Buck O'Neil had been the Jackie Robinson of coaching—the first Black coach in the major league. (He'd also played with Jackie Robinson on the Monarchs in 1945.)

I had heard of the Negro Leagues, because I'd watched

Ken Burns's baseball documentary a couple years earlier. But my awareness didn't extend much beyond the obvious marquee names, like Satchel Paige, Jackie Robinson, and Hank Aaron—players who became stars in the majors. My interest started to build. Then, a new set of baseball cards from Topps took it to the next level.

In 2006, the card company issued a set called Topps Allen & Ginter, which was a throwback reference to an original line of cigarette cards by that name, first released in the late 1880s. The Allen & Ginter cards in 2006 featured a wide range of popular figures including wrestler Hulk Hogan, basketball player Dennis Rodman, race car driver Danica Patrick, and soccer star Mia Hamm, in addition to baseball players.

In 2007, Topps released a second set of Allen & Ginter cards, which included a handful of Negro League players whose names I wasn't familiar with, in part because most of them hadn't ever been featured on an official baseball card before. One of the cards featured a player named John "Mule" Miles. Miles had played with the Chicago American Giants from 1946 to 1949, and became legendary after he hit a home run in eleven straight games. He got his colorful nickname because a coach said he "hit like a mule kicks." As part of Major League Baseball's efforts to redeem itself with late recognition of historically significant Negro League stars, each of the thirty major-league teams "drafted" a former Negro League player on June 5, 2008. Miles—who also was a member of the famed Tuskegee Airmen during World War II—got picked by the Seattle Mariners.

COMEBACK SEASON

I took a look at the SportsCollectors.Net website, and found a record of just one person who said they had sent a letter to a former Negro Leaguer in the Allen & Ginter set. He said the player had been ecstatic to receive it. I thought that sounded cool, and since I now had John "Mule" Miles's card from the set, I figured I'd try my hand at reaching out to him. I sent him a letter along with some money and a few of his baseball cards, which I asked him to sign.

John responded with a letter that read:

Dec. 29, 2007

Hello Cam:

Thank you for the donation and such a nice letter. I love hearing from baseball fans.

Yes I had an amazing baseball career, hitting home runs and winning ball games. There were tears, joys, triumphs and laughter as we played the game. All of that did not hamper us (the players) at any time. We never had huge salaries, like the players of today. We played for the love of the game. I do not have any regrets. Have signed your cards, as you requested. Yes I know all the players from the Texas Negro League. I am sending you a Roy White card. It is the only player that I had to send you.

Best of luck with your collection. It was nice to hear from you. Happy holidays.

John "Mule" Miles

JOHN 'MULE' MILES.
ALLEN & GINTER'S
BROOKLYN. 2007 NEW YORK.

The autographed 2007 Topps Allen & Ginter card, sent to me by John "Mule" Miles during my first personal exchange with a former player from the Negro Leagues.

This was a big moment for me. John had written a meaningful reply instead of simply signing the card and sending it back. It reminded me of the personal connection I'd felt when I got the letter back from Red Borom. But this was even better. There was history, yes, but there was also a sense of having gotten to speak with someone others had overlooked. I'll admit that as a thirteen-year-old I didn't have the strongest sense of race, and certainly not of historical and systemic racial injustice, but I could sense that there was something deeply unfair in the way John "Mule" Miles and other Black ballplayers had been treated. And yet, right there in his letter, there was also this defiant, inspiring pride: "All of that did not hamper us," he'd written. "We never had huge salaries, like the players of today. We played for the love of the game. I do not have any regrets." I wouldn't have been able to put the reasons why into words at the time, but I was hooked.

I decided to invest in a book of addresses for professional athletes put out by a guy named Harvey Meiselman. The book cost $35, which was a lot of money for me at the time. There were thousands of addresses of professional athletes in there, but what drew me to it most was that there was a small Negro Leagues section with about one hundred or so names.

I got a few replies after writing letters to players on the list, but it wasn't long until I ran into a wall. Through talking on internet forums with other people interested in the Negro Leagues, I realized that at least half the addresses were outdated. In some cases, the listed player had even, sadly, passed away. The Meiselman list was a start, but it seemed that nobody was doing a good enough job of keeping up with these guys. If a former MLB player passed away, Wikipedia would be updated immediately. If a Negro League player had passed away three years prior, there might not even be an obituary for him in his local newspaper.

Sitting in my room one evening, I had a revelation: there must be a ton of former Negro League players from the forties, fifties, and early sixties who were still alive, somewhere out there. If it was possible to find all of those "cup of coffee" players, as I'd done, then it must be possible for someone to locate these former Negro Leaguers. And I was the one who could do it.

It was like the proverbial lightbulb had been switched on. I had a new project that would quickly grow into an obsession: find and contact every former Negro League player who was still alive in America.

Around this time, I fortuitously stumbled onto an online forum specifically for the Negro Leagues, organized by the Negro League Baseball Players Association (NLBPA). The organization had been founded by a couple of former players in Philadelphia. The players did events and made appearances in the Philly area, so the forum was a way for people to get in contact with them as well as discuss anything else pertaining to the leagues. One of the players, Stanley Glenn, who was also president of the NLBPA board of directors, had a card in the Allen & Ginter set. When I wrote to him, he sent me back a flyer for his book that he had just published, *Don't Let Anyone Take Your Joy Away: An Inside Look at Negro League Baseball and Its Legacy*. Glenn had been a catcher for the Philadelphia Stars and said one of the highlights of his career was catching for Satchel Paige. I sent him money for the book and he sent back an autographed copy, which I excitedly read right away. It was an eye-opening look at the trials of playing baseball in the Jim Crow South in the 1940s.

The NLBPA forum was a rudimentary-looking website without any log-in required, but it was a source of endless hours of delight for me. Since anybody could post something, and the posts never went away, I could read posts going all the way back to when the site was launched eight years earlier in 1999. Over that span people had been asking for all kinds of stuff—like information on Buck O'Neil's career for a middle school paper or a mailing address for a particular player.

I put up a few posts myself, looking for others who collected autographs of Negro League players. This is when I began to make crucial contacts with several guys who had a passion for the Negro Leagues and who became guides or mentors to me. I slowly became a well-known entity in this tiny circle. I established an email relationship with Wayne Stivers, a researcher in his sixties who would give me players' addresses. He was a little particular about the way he did things—he'd only dole out a few addresses at a time. He also sold me different players' autographs for $7 to $10 each. But he always had good intentions, and he taught me a lot. If I sent Wayne an email asking if he knew of any players from the Memphis Red Sox, he would send me a few players' addresses, with the admonition that I send the players $5 when asking for their autograph, because he said that many of them were in dire financial circumstances.

While I was sending letters to players, I was also reaching out to other collectors to trade autographs. If they had an autograph of a Negro League player who was no longer alive, I would send them one of the duplicate autographs I had gotten, in a straight trade. In this way, I could expand my collection without having to shell out money, since I still didn't have much of that.

One day, we got a phone call to the house from a guy asking to speak to "Lauren Perron." He said that someone with her account on eBay had bought an autographed photo of a Negro Leaguer from him. Since eBay is supposed to be a confidential platform, my mom was kind of freaked out. She finally gave me the phone when she understood who he was and why he was calling. His name was Gary Crawford and he was a collector in his mid-fifties who had recently started a nonprofit to try to help out former Negro Leaguers by getting them booked for public appearances and events where they could be paid. He was curious about this person in Massachusetts interested enough in the Negro Leagues to purchase an autograph from him—it was that rare of an occurrence.

Up until this point, I'd received a few letters back from Negro League players in which they gave me their phone numbers. I'd called and we'd had brief conversations. But a player named Al Barks and I seemed to have a real connection. We chatted at length a couple of times. He shared his memories of playing for the Black Yankees, and told stories about his former teammates. He spoke to me like I was an adult, not the thirteen-year-old that I was. It was the thing I'd always wanted, back from the time I was in preschool.

I had a couple of other little thrills that intensified my interest in tracking more players down. On the NLBPA forum, I'd seen a post from a former player named Reginald Howard. Howard had been a batboy for Negro League games that came through his hometown of South Bend, Indiana, during the leagues' heyday in the 1940s. He then had become a player himself for the Indianapolis Clowns in the 1950s. I reached out to Howard by email asking if he would be willing to sign an autograph for me, and he responded to say that his rule was he wouldn't sign autographs for people without meeting them in person. The thing was, he lived in Memphis, Tennessee.

Howard later said that he was suspicious when I first reached out to him.

"I thought it was probably somebody hustling, trying to get autographs to sell," Howard said. "People exploit Black men."

When I let him know I lived in the Boston area and I was thirteen years old, he changed his mind. Howard and I got to know each other over the phone and established a relationship. He saw that he could trust me. In addition to agreeing to sign an autograph for me, he actually asked if I could help him with a website he was creating and put out "feelers" to get him more speaking engagements. I was thrilled because it was the first time a player had asked me to do something for him. The idea that he thought I had the ability to help was a major boost to my self-confidence and my sense of what possibilities were out there as I continued to reach out to former players from the Negro Leagues.

Howard also sent me an old clipping in the mail that listed the names of his teammates on the 1956 Clowns. I got a jolt when I saw the name Al Barks on the list. This was the same Al Barks I had gotten in touch with, and spoken with on the phone. I realized that Howard had no idea that Al Barks was still alive or where he was. I sent Barks a copy of the clipping and gave him Howard's number. I urged him to give his old teammate Reggie Howard a call, and he did. They both told me how happy they were to reconnect.

It was another big moment in which I felt like I could be of service to these men, this time helping them resurrect relationships with long-lost friends and teammates. That was becoming far more gratifying for me than just collecting autographs.

I recently asked Reggie Howard if he would share some reflections on his career, and he was kind enough to do so:

My first exposure to baseball was through an uncle who had a semipro career. On Sundays, my brother and I would go out with him when we were six and seven years old and do the things little boys do to help baseball teams—gather balls, hand bats to players. Then I started to play organized ball,

Little League, at age ten. As I began to evolve, people thought I had certain attributes that maybe I didn't have, pegging me as a future pro from such a young age. I started to play with another semipro team in my teens and I began to blossom. I played mostly second base.

I lived and breathed baseball. Blacks are not playing baseball today, but as you remember, when I came up that's all we had. There was nobody in the NFL and the NBA. The only thing Blacks had was baseball and boxing. That's why I played baseball.

When Jackie Robinson joined the Dodgers, it had a significant positive impact on me. We were boys. As the Bible says: when I was a child I spoke as a child, I thought as a child, I did childish things, but when I became a man I threw away childish thoughts. When Jackie first signed I was happy like everybody else. I didn't realize the sophisticated parts of it. J. B. Martin, who you don't know, was owner of the Chicago American Giants and president of the Negro American League. His philosophy was to take the entire Negro Leagues, twelve teams, and consolidate those teams down to eight teams, four in the American League and four in the National League. It made all the sense in the world, but the way it was structured was to raid the Negro Leagues of their players and never compensate anybody. In other words, the Dodgers didn't pay J. L. Wilkinson, owner of the Kansas City Monarchs, one penny for Jackie Robinson. They didn't pay one penny for Johnny Wright. They just took the players. I didn't look at it with any hatred, but

51

I thought it was wrongly implemented. And it destroyed the Negro League, which was the second-largest money-producing business in the country for Blacks at the time. They never compensated any owners. I had some disdain for that part.

When I was a kid, about eleven and twelve, I was a batboy for the Black teams that came to South Bend to play the Studebakers. I saw the Negro Leagues in its heyday. I saw Jackie Robinson when he was a shortstop for KC, Monte Irvin and Larry Doby on the Newark Eagles. I saw all of them. On game day it was a huge event for the Black community. But I was just a child.

When I started playing the league was breaking down. It was tearing up. I played a couple years for the Clowns. What happened is, they couldn't pay salaries because the star players were being taken away by the major league so your attendance was down. People were going to minor-league and major-league games instead of the Negro Leagues. The guys who were older, like over twenty-seven, were married and had children. We couldn't play in the league anymore because we didn't make enough money to stay. So guys started going to semipro teams, in Canada and anywhere else they could play. The Negro Leagues turned into a developmental league. The caliber of ball watered down significantly from what it was when I was a batboy.

My memories that stand out from the Clowns are just playing ball every day. It was hard, riding in the bus. I enjoyed it and I didn't enjoy it, if that makes sense. I enjoyed traveling to places and meeting people. I didn't enjoy the conditions in which we traveled, the hotels we stayed in. At some point I realized I wasn't going to go much further in baseball.

After he had reconnected with Al Barks, Reggie Howard mentioned to me that there were two other former teammates he was interested in finding, Roger Daniels and Gilbert Black. Both of those players' names were on the clipping

Reginald Howard (*first row, fourth from left*) as a young batboy at the 1947 Negro League East–West All-Star Game at Comiskey Park, Chicago.

he'd sent me of the '56 Indianapolis Clowns. I asked Wayne Stivers, the researcher I'd met online, about the names. He told me he had interviewed Daniels a decade earlier, and gave me his contact information. When I called the number, I was pleased to get him on the phone, to make yet another contact I could pass on to Reggie Howard. Daniels said he hadn't talked to any of his former teammates in many years. Like Howard, Daniels said he was particularly interested in talking to Gilbert Black, who he said was his best friend on the Clowns. He said he hadn't seen Black in almost thirty years.

I undertook the mission to locate Gilbert Black. I used my usual methods of locating people, diving into corners of the internet, and was able to pick up enough information to be reasonably confident that he was currently living in Connecticut. Then, I rifled through online phone directories and called anyone I could find in Connecticut with that name. I called at least two dozen numbers, with no luck. One day, I was poking around on the NLBPA forum and I saw a post from a woman who said her dad had played in the Negro Leagues. I sent her an email asking his name.

"Gilbert Black," she said in her reply.

My eyes bulged.

"Is he the Gilbert Black that lives in Connecticut?" I asked.

"Yes," she replied. "Here's his number."

I had been calling and calling, looking for him. I had begun to lose hope. I had even been told by one person that Gilbert Black was dead. Clearly, they had been talking about another person with the same name, because here he was, introduced to me by his own daughter. It was a crazy bit of luck. I called Gilbert and had a great chat with him. Then I put him in contact with Reggie Howard and Roger Daniels.

I sent an email to Wayne, describing the sequence of events that led to me tracking down Gilbert Black.

"Wayne, I want to get some credit for this," I said, proud of my work. "I just found a Negro League player that I'm one hundred percent sure nobody's ever interviewed before."

Wayne agreed. He put a notice in the Negro League research newsletter that came out every few months. It wasn't exactly the *New York Times*—its circulation was a small group of researchers around the country interested in the Negro Leagues—but to me, it might as well have been.

I was thirteen, and all I wanted to do was locate former Negro League players, help them in any way I could, and connect them to their old teammates. Each contact was leading me to others, like a giant jigsaw puzzle. It was all immensely appealing to my thirteen-year-old brain. It gave me direction. To add to the sense of responsibility, importance, and excitement, I saw the task of locating guys as a race against time, because I knew they were aging and could be gone at any moment.

There were now days when I would spend four or five hours on the phone talking to these former players, from the moment I got home from school to well into the night.

Thankfully, my family continued to support me. They saw how much it mattered to me, and how good I would feel whenever I located a new player. Even when things didn't go quite as planned, I wasn't deterred, and my family stuck by me. For example, we went to a family function in New York City, and I had never been more excited because I had arranged to meet Roger Daniels—the former Indianapolis Clowns player who had been friends with Reginald Howard and Gilbert Black. While my mom, brothers, and grandmother went out shopping and walking around Times Square, my dad and I planned to go to Harlem to meet Daniels. We had agreed on a time with him, but the exact place hadn't yet been determined. An hour or so before the time we were supposed to meet, I called him; he answered and said he would call me back shortly. He never did. I kept calling Roger back and couldn't get ahold of him. He stood me up! I never did find out why, or get the chance to meet him.

Other challenges were a little more fundamental, and hurtful. A lot of my parents' friends didn't get why I was so interested in the Negro Leagues. Some of them were confused about why a kid wouldn't want to be outside playing baseball or at a friend's house playing Xbox. Normal kids don't get obsessed with research—I get that. Others, however, seemed more fixated on race. My parents said that a couple of their friends asked, "Why is he only interested in the Black leagues?" Even my grandmother, on my mom's side, once asked: "What is with Cam and all these Black baseball players?" My parents tried to explain about the history of the Negro Leagues, the way players were mistreated, and how meaningful I found it to talk to them. Some of the people who were confused got it, many others didn't, but to my everlasting gratitude, both of my parents did their part to speak up for what was right, and always stood with me.

CHAPTER 4

The History of Black Baseball in America

Before going any further, I'd like to give some background on the too-little-known but absolutely incredible history of Black baseball in America. It's a story that's brought to life by fascinating people, and a big part of my own life has been devoted to learning everything that I can about them.

Before the Civil War, the fledgling sport of "base ball," as it was known at the time, was played mostly by white, wealthy gentlemen amateurs. But during the war, it spread via army camps and military prisons to the wider population, and in the postwar era, it gained in popularity. To my surprise when I first learned it, there was a brief period of racial integration in baseball during this time in the late 1800s. It was far from perfect, but there were more than sixty Black players who played in white leagues between the end of the Civil War and the turn of the century, according to Robert Peterson, one of the first chroniclers of Black baseball, in his book *Only the Ball Was White: A History of Legendary Black Players and All-Black Professional Teams*.

This period also coincided with the professionalization of baseball. In 1876, the National League of Professional Base Ball Clubs was established, which marks the start of American baseball becoming organized and beginning to resemble the professional structure we know today. The National League started out with eight teams.

The earliest Black professional baseball player was Bud Fowler. Fowler was a tall infielder from Cooperstown, New York—which is often called the birthplace of baseball, though it's now well established that this isn't really true. But that's another story. Fowler was playing second base for a professional team in New Castle, Pennsylvania, in 1872 when he was only fourteen years old, according to some accounts—though others claim he didn't play until a few years later. At any rate, Fowler appears to have been the first Black person to be paid to play baseball.

Fowler bounced around America and Canada for the next twenty-five years, playing primarily for teams in what was called the International League, in such far-flung locales as Minnesota, Massachusetts, Iowa, and Ontario, Canada. Though the teams he played for were technically integrated (since he was on them), he was a continual target of racism. In one instance, the Maple Leafs in Ontario released him because some of the team's white players refused to play with him. Yet there was no question about his skills on the field. In the pages of the popular weekly American newspaper *Sporting Life*, Fowler was called "one of the best players in the country."

Another early Black pioneer of the sport was the good-looking, well-educated Moses Fleetwood "Fleet" Walker, who was the son of an Ohio doctor. Fleet Walker played in 1884 with the Toledo Blue Stockings, a team that had just joined a rival professional league to the National League, known as the American Association. Fleet's brother Weldy played a few games for the Blue Stockings as well. But when Toledo ventured south to play against Richmond, Fleet Walker received a letter stating that he would be swarmed by a mob of seventy-five white men if he played that day. The letter didn't stop him from playing, but it seemed his teammates weren't so brave, and looked for a way to get rid of him. In 1885, they saw an opportunity to release him after he cracked a rib—not exactly a career-ending injury.

It should be noted that as far back as 1860—just fourteen years after the first officially recorded baseball game—Black players were already coming together to play baseball without looking for the acceptance of whites or waiting for white teams to "integrate" them. On September 28, 1860, according to baseball historian Harry Simmons, a Black team from Weeksville, New York, played a game against the Colored Union Club at Brooklyn's Elysian Fields, the first recorded game played by two Black teams (and won by Weeksville, 11–0).

There were various efforts in the 1880s to form a league of all-Black teams, but none came to fruition until the creation of the Southern League. The Southern League was an organized group of ten teams, and kicked off in June 1886 with a game in New Orleans between the Eclipse of Memphis and the Unions of New Orleans. (The Eclipse won, 3–1.) But the league's success was short-lived. When a massive earthquake struck Charleston, South Carolina, on August 31, 1886, the damage was so great that the league had to shut down. To this day, it's still one of the most powerful earthquakes the East Coast has ever had—sixty people died, two thousand buildings were damaged, and the shock was felt in an area spanning from Boston, to Chicago, to New Orleans, to Cuba.

The most successful Black team during these early years wasn't part of any particular league, and had complicated, painful origins. They were called the Cuban Giants, but as Mark Ribowsky wrote in *A Complete History of the Negro Leagues, 1884 to 1955*, they "were about as Cuban as chitlins." They were originally a collection of Black waiters and porters at the Argyle Hotel on Long Island in New York, who played games to entertain the white patrons. A vacationing white businessman from Trenton, New Jersey, named Walter Cook, saw them play and came up with the idea to pretend they were Hispanic to entertain and attract white fans.

"Bounding onto the field, they would chirp pidgin *español* and cackle loudly, in a gross parody of everybody's idea of how Hispanics acted," Ribowsky wrote. "Not through a con but by playing superb baseball, by 1887 the Cubans had attained a level of notoriety that gave them the right to pick and choose which white teams they would play."

The Cubans barnstormed across the Northeast, beating all comers, even coming close to beating the National League champion Detroit Wolverines (though they wound up losing 5–2 when they made four errors in the last two innings).

By 1889, the National League and the American Association, the two most prominent white leagues, were drawing more than 2 million fans a year to their games. Each league had eight teams, and together they covered the country's major cities. These were the leagues that would begin cooperating with each other in 1903, marking what we now consider the official start of Major League Baseball. As money became a bigger factor, a desire grew among white players—many of whom were first-generation Irish and German immigrants desperate for a paycheck—to formally exclude Blacks. This effort was led by one of the game's stars, Adrian "Cap" Anson, a racist from Iowa who had become a national idol. The International League, the one in which Fleet Walker and Bud Fowler played, soon voted to ban Black players as well. Walker and his brother left the game, opened a hotel in Ohio, and went on to publish a Black newspaper, the *Equator*. The superb Frank Grant, who had played for the International League team the Buffalo Bisons, in Buffalo, New York, went on to play for the Cuban Giants.

This is what an unnamed white player in the International League told the *Sporting News* in 1889 about what the Black players faced:

While I myself am prejudiced against playing in a team with a colored player, still I could not help pitying some of the poor black fellows that played in the International League. Fowler used to play second base with the lower part of his legs encased in wooden guards. He knew that about every player that came down to second base on a steal had it in for him and would, if possible, throw the spikes into him. He was a good player, but left the base every time there was a close play in order to get away from the spikes.

I have seen him muff balls intentionally, so that he would not have to try to touch runners, fearing they might injure him. [Frank] Grant was the same way. Why, the runners chased him off second base. They went down so often trying to break his legs or injure them that he gave up his infield position the latter part of last season and played right field. This is not all.

About half the pitchers try their best to hit these colored players when at bat. I know of a great many pitchers that tried to soak Grant. . . . One of the International League pitchers pitched for Grant's head all the time. He never put a ball over the plate but sent them in straight and true right at Grant. Do what he would he could not hit the Buffalo man, and he [Grant] trotted down to first on called balls all the time.

As it was, *Sporting Life* credited the invention of baseball's first shin guards to Grant—a sobering thought about the origins of this piece of equipment. Players also credited Grant with the invention of the feet-first slide, by association and inadvertently: because opposing players had started to slide that way, with their spikes raised, to try to hurt him.

The Jim Crow laws and system had firmly taken hold of the South by the start of the twentieth century, and Black players had no choice but to form their own professional leagues. So, as with many things, necessity became the mother of invention. Over the next half century, reflecting the precarious economic fortunes of the Black community, these Black leagues and teams that collectively make up the Negro Leagues would constantly struggle to make enough money to cover expenses and pay players a livable wage. But what the leagues and teams lacked in financial sustainability and top-down structure, they more than made up for in exciting, stylish play on the field; nurturing and growing bona fide superstars; and passionate fan bases who loved to see their teams play.

Organized Black baseball at the turn of the century was at first dominated by five professional teams that competed fiercely against one another. There were two teams from the New York City area, the Cuban Giants and the Cuban X Giants (a bit confusing, I know); two teams from Chicago, the Chicago Unions and the Columbia Giants; and the Red Stockings of Norfolk, Virginia. With the exception of the Red Stockings, the teams were clustered in the areas where millions of Black people had been migrating in order to escape the brutality of the Jim Crow South. By 1910, many more professional Black teams were springing up all over the place, and various efforts were made to form them into an organized and regulated national league.

It would be left to one man to exert his enormous will on the scattered teams and bring them together: Andrew "Rube" Foster. Born in Texas in 1879, the large, imposing Foster started out as a dominating pitcher for the Chicago Union Giants (formed by a merger between the earlier-mentioned Chicago Unions and Columbia Giants). He blew away hitters in the fledgling Negro Leagues with a blazing fastball and unhittable screwball—then known as the "fadeaway." Foster is credited with a fifty-one-win season as pitcher for the Cuban X Giants in 1902, leading them to the fabled "Colored World Championship." After he formed his own club, the Chicago American Giants, in 1910, Foster perfected a new style of baseball that he'd been developing over the previous three years as the field manager of the Leland Giants. His version of the game used speed, daring base-running, and powerful pitching to dominate opponents, and would soon come to change the entire sport.

This is how Mark Ribowsky described it in *A Complete History of the Negro Leagues*:

The hit-and-run play had long been a part of the game, but Foster, a brilliant manager, made it nearly the whole game. Everybody ran, breaking from first on nearly every pitch. This whirl of men in motion drove pitchers nutty, and Foster tortured them further by playing bunt-and-run, which meant that, when the strategy was executed correctly, a man could go first to third without the ball being hit beyond the pitcher's mound.

The Leland Giants were indoctrinated to take the extra base, and a dawdling fielder could prove fatal to his team's chances. Knowing that this fielder would overcompensate by hurrying his throw, Foster could reasonably expect to score extra runs on errors. Foster also instructed his men to wait out the pitcher, rattling the man's nerves. And his own pitchers were schooled in Rube's rules of geometry, physics, and psychology; often, the slightest alteration in a man's windup or stride to the plate could make him a winner, and Rube studied his pitchers from top to bottom, looking for structural flaws.

Foster's teams were so formidable that the white major-league teams generally avoided playing them, thinking they had much to lose and little to gain. But by many accounts, white major leaguers would join Foster's Chicago teams on the sly, picking up spare cash by pulling their hats far down over their faces and using a pseudonym.

In February 1920, Foster brought the owners of the top Negro clubs in the Midwest together in Kansas City to decide on the particulars for a new league, the Negro National League. The first game was played in Indianapolis on May 2, with the Indianapolis ABCs beating Joe Green's Chicago Giants, 4–2.

In *Heroes of the Negro Leagues* by Mark Chiarello and Jack

Andrew "Rube" Foster, founder and first president of the Negro National League.

Morelli, they write that Foster, as president of the NNL, "ran it like the Majors."

"He increased interest and attendance by holding organized pennant races and introducing All-Star Games, raised equipment standards, and assured players regular paychecks for set amounts—while drawing no salary himself. Foreseeing the eventual end to racial segregation, Foster counseled his athletes to maintain a high level of play. 'When the doors are opened, you must be ready to walk through' was his advice."

Foster was occasionally even surreptitiously called upon by major-league clubs to work with their pitchers. He was a brilliant trailblazer, and his historical impact has now rightfully come to be seen as being on par with the greatest Black artists and intellectuals of the time. As Rutgers historian Clement Price says in Lawrence D. Hogan's book *Shades of Glory: The Negro Leagues and the Story of African-American Baseball*, "In the early 20th century . . . Negro baseball surfaces as an important symbol of black accomplishment in the cities, black accomplishment on the playing field, and black business development. The New Negro Era, long known for its poets and its jazz musicians and its intellectuals, must now be reconsidered for its sports figures."

In December 1923, six Black teams from the East, led by Ed Bolden and his Hilldales out of Philadelphia, and the white booking agent Nat Strong, who owned the Brooklyn Royal Giants, came together to form the Eastern Colored League. A national rivalry between the Eastern Colored League and the Negro National League was born—enhanced by Rube Foster's and Nat Strong's personal dislike for each other. The rivalry would be marked by the leagues raiding each other for top players and heightened by the champs of each league competing directly against each other in a Black World Series, launched in 1924 and won that year by the Kansas City Monarchs. Established in 1920 by J. L. Wilkinson, the first white owner in the leagues, the Monarchs would become perhaps the most storied franchise in the history of the Negro Leagues. They would sign and develop Jackie Robinson, and ultimately send more players to MLB teams than any other Negro League franchise, including the great Satchel Paige, Ernie Banks, Elston Howard, Hank Thompson, Buck O'Neil, and Gene Baker. The Monarchs were also responsible for a number of innovations, including the portable lighting system, which they would drive from city to city in trucks, allowing them to play night games—five years before any MLB team.

After Rube Foster died of a heart attack in December 1930, his Negro National League soon collapsed. This was a huge loss. But the league would be successfully reorganized under the same name, in 1934, in the midst of the Great Depression.

The Negro Leagues of this era saw the rise of two enormous talents, Satchel Paige and Josh Gibson, who would become superstars and household names in the Black community. There are so many mythical stories about these two men that it becomes hard to know what to believe. With both, the legends begin and end with their extraordinary, once-in-a-century talent.

Leroy "Satchel" Paige was born in Mobile, Alabama, in 1906—though he was always circumspect about exactly how old he was. He picked up the moniker "Satchel" when he was a young man working as a baggage porter at Mobile's train station, and devised a system of carrying several satchels at once on a long pole. He possessed a magical right arm that could throw a baseball harder and truer than perhaps any other person in the twentieth century. Tall at six-four, but skinny at 150 pounds, Satchel also had a devil-may-care personality that was considerably enhanced by his talent for showmanship. From the time he joined the Birmingham Black Barons in 1928 and over a career that would span, incredibly, the next four decades, fans—Black and white—simply couldn't get enough of him. Though there were some Black people who didn't appreciate his ways, thinking he was not a good representative of the community.

"Paige's slow gait, his double-whammy, double-pump windups, even his habit of getting to the park at the last minute, if at all, may be construed today as pandering to an Uncle Tom image of how white America saw people of color and how blacks saw themselves in a looking glass warped by the feeble-minded movie roles Hollywood seemed to reserve for African-Americans," wrote Ribowsky in *A Complete History of the Negro Leagues*. "On the other hand, his act could have been a send-up of that debased sensibility. Whatever it was to the cultural mindset of the twenties and thirties, for Satchel Paige it held one purpose: to make a buck and a name for himself."

Satchel used his fame as a powerful negotiating tool—if he didn't get paid the amount he wanted from the team he was supposed to be playing for, there were times when he decided not to show up and instead went to pitch for somebody who was paying more. It was a practice Satchel continued for most of his career, eventually forcing the owner of whatever Negro League team he was on at the time to consent to occasionally renting out his services to the highest bidder.

In *Only the Ball Was White*, Robert Peterson estimated that Paige earned three to four times as much money as any other player in Black baseball, with a salary that reached as high as $40,000 a year with the Kansas City Monarchs (which would be close to a million dollars in 2020).

Leroy "Satchel" Paige playing for the Kansas City Monarchs.

In a story about Satchel of the more mythical variety, famed Negro League catcher Biz Mackey once said Satchel threw the ball so hard that sometimes it just seemed to disappear.

"Yes, disappear. I've heard about Satchel throwing pitches that wasn't hit but that never showed up in the catcher's mitt nevertheless," Mackey said. "They say the catcher, the umpire, and the bat boy looked all over for that ball, but it was gone. Now how do you account for that?"

A year after Jackie Robinson was signed by the Dodgers,

breaking through the major league's color line, Bill Veeck signed Satchel—at this point in his forties—to the Cleveland Indians. The oldest rookie in major-league history, Satchel drew 201,829 fans for his first three starts, setting night-game attendance records in Cleveland and Chicago. He ended the season with a record of 6-1—he even had a couple of base hits—and was voted Rookie of the Year by the *Sporting News*. He then made an appearance in Cleveland's World Series win over the Boston Braves, thus becoming the first Black pitcher to pitch in a World Series game.

In 1965, at age fifty-nine (maybe), Satchel pitched three innings of one-hit ball for the Kansas City Athletics, closing out one of the most mind-bending sports careers in history. Satchel died on June 8, 1982—living long enough to see Academy Award–winning actor Louis Gossett Jr. play him in a 1981 made-for-television movie, *Don't Look Back*, based on his autobiography of the same name.

While Satchel was the showman, Josh Gibson preferred to let his bat do the talking. At a hulking and muscular six-one, 215 pounds, Gibson hit balls so far that he was dubbed "the Black Babe Ruth." Gibson hit seventy-five home runs in 1931 with the Homestead Grays, and sixty-nine in 1934 with the Pittsburgh Crawfords. According to Chiarello and Morelli's *Heroes of the Negro Leagues*, Gibson hit a home run one out of every dozen times at the plate—and was the only hitter to blast a ball out of Yankee Stadium, landing on a Bronx street.

Gibson continued to play—and hit home runs—for two years after he was diagnosed in 1943 with a possible brain tumor. On January 20, 1947, Gibson went to sleep and never woke up. His death came just two months before Jackie Robinson's historic debut with the Brooklyn Dodgers.

Libraries full of books have been written about Jackie Robinson, whom Chiarello and Morelli called "Dr. King in cleats." After starring as a four-sport athlete at UCLA, best known for his skill on the football field (he was an all-American), Robinson joined the Kansas City Monarchs in 1945. He played just forty-seven games—with a .387 average and thirteen stolen bases—before Brooklyn Dodgers owner Branch Rickey decided that Jackie was the man he had been looking for to break through the color line.

Far fewer words have been written about the effect Robinson's signing had on the fortunes of the Negro Leagues. Once the gate was opened, major-league teams were free to use the Negro Leagues as a training ground, cherrypicking top players without having to worry about seasoning them with extended stays in the minor leagues. It was a process that Negro League owners encouraged—the cash they got from major-league teams was money they could use to sustain their clubs for another season. But the on-field product suffered mightily—as did interest from Black fans, who now were closely following the fortunes of Black players in the major league. One of the most damaging blows was the abandonment of the Black press. For decades, they had been the most loyal chroniclers of the daily matchups and machinations of Black baseball, but the Black press abruptly shifted its interests and coverage to the major league.

"The most talented players, especially the young guys with a future, were being bought—poached, really—by the Major League teams," wrote former player Stanley Glenn in his book *Don't Let Anyone Take Your Joy Away*. "If it meant ignoring contracts they were already signed under, so be it. Once that happened, we started to lose our fan base, because everybody liked to go to Major League ballparks. They figured that's where you were going to see the best. After the 1947 season, I started wondering if the majors didn't mean to destroy us."

Due to plunging attendance and large financial losses, the New York Black Yankees disbanded and the Newark Eagles—a team that played in the Negro National League starting in 1936, and had many great players including Leon Day, Larry Doby, Monte Irvin, and Biz Mackey—were sold at the end of the 1948 season. (A photo of Leon Day and some of his Newark Eagles teammates is featured on the cover of this book.) The Homestead Grays returned to barnstorming, bringing an end to the sixteen-year run of the reorganized Negro National League that had originally started back with Rube Foster. The Grays played and won the 1948 Negro World Series against the Birmingham Black Barons in near obscurity, since few papers covered it—the *Pittsburgh Courier* noted the win in a two-paragraph story buried under a series about Blacks in the major league. It would be the final Negro World Series ever played.

The remaining teams joined the Negro American League, with the Eastern Division made up of the New York Cubans, Baltimore Elite Giants, Philadelphia Stars, Indianapolis Clowns, and Louisville Buckeyes, and the Western Division of the Kansas City Monarchs, Chicago American Giants, Memphis Red Sox, Birmingham Black Barons, and Houston Eagles (formerly the Newark Eagles).

By 1952, the league was down to six teams. The title that year was won by the Clowns, who used gimmickry and comedy to increase fan interest—though some Blacks found the comic routines of figures like "King Tut," "Peanuts," "Goose" Tatum (who also starred for the comedic Harlem Globetrotters basketball team), and the dwarf "Spec Bebop" to be offensive. The Clowns also played three women in the infield during the 1950s—Toni Stone, who played in 1953 until she was traded to the Monarchs, then Connie Morgan and Mamie "Peanut" Johnson in 1954.

According to Alan J. Pollock's book about his father's years as owner of the Clowns, *Barnstorming to Heaven: Syd Pollock and His Great Black Teams*, the team's quality of play, as well as the league's, was rapidly diminishing in 1952, when they heard of a seventeen-year-old kid in Mobile, Alabama, who might be able to fill the team's need at shortstop. The scrawny young shortstop's name was Henry "Hank" Aaron—and he needed the approval of his parents to join the team and accept a salary of $200, because he wasn't yet eighteen. After observing Aaron's already breathtaking hitting ability, Syd Pollock raised his salary to $250. Aaron soon was given the nickname "Pork Chop," because he seemed to eat them for every meal.

When the eighteen-year-old Aaron left the Clowns on

June 15 after Pollock sold his contract to the Braves for $10,000, he was leading the Negro American League in batting, runs, doubles, home runs, RBIs, and total bases. After spending the balance of 1952 and 1953 in the Braves' farm system, Aaron joined the big-league club as a starter in spring 1954, when outfielder Bobby Thomson broke his ankle—the first step in one of the greatest major-league baseball careers of all time.

From the early 1950s until the mid-1960s, Black professional baseball survived, and the Negro National League remained, but not without a struggle. Major-league teams continued to integrate their organizations bit by bit, poaching top talent from Negro League teams, and Negro League fan attendance continued to drop. What had been the Negro Leagues' pinnacle event, the East–West All-Star Game, went from a two-game, multicity spectacle with more than 85,000 fans in combined attendance in 1947, to a one-game showcase with a turnout of 7,500 a decade later. (A great player who would later become my friend, Joe Elliott, played for the Birmingham Black Barons in that 1957 All-Star Game, and lost.)

By 1959, the Boston Red Sox made an infamous bit of history by becoming the very last MLB team to integrate, with the debut of Elijah "Pumpsie" Green. In 1962, the diminished Negro American League finally folded after what would be the very last East-West All-Star Game. The following year, even though there was no "official" league, several teams continued to play independent barnstorming schedules. But when the Monarchs hung up their cleats in 1965, the Negro Leagues were really and truly gone. Ironically, by the time the Clowns, which kept on going as an unaffiliated endeavor barnstorming the country, disbanded in the early 1980s, the team was all white.

Just as school integration after the 1954 *Brown v. Board of Education* decision brought with it a raft of problems that have now plagued African-American students for several generations, the death of the Negro Leagues spelled the end of an era that many saw as a shining example of African-American excellence.

"I think a lot was lost when the Negro Leagues went belly up," pioneering and award-winning writer John Edgar Wideman, a top college basketball player himself, said in the book *Shades of Glory*. "I think a lot was lost when the black colleges began to lose students and funds. After all, this is supposed to be a culture, a society, of diversity. And losing institutions that have that long a life and play that crucial a role in the community . . . it's very worrisome. . . . What was contained in those institutions was not simply a black version of what white people were doing, but the game was played differently."

"But what we gained was greater," pioneering Black journalist Mal Goode countered in the same book. "We got our self-respect, and you have to be black to understand what that meant."

In his autobiography, *I Was Right on Time: My Journey from the Negro Leagues to the Majors*, former Kansas City Monarchs star and major-league manager Buck O'Neil said he gets a "bittersweet feeling" when he thinks about what happened to the Black community after Robinson joined the Dodgers.

COMEBACK SEASON

"A lot of people lost their whole way of life," O'Neil wrote. "That was another of those ironies, the hardest one. Not only did a black business die, other black businesses did, too, the ones that were dependent on black baseball and black entertainment. . . . A way of life came to an end along with black baseball. But I guess it couldn't be any other way."

CHAPTER 5

Seeing the Hard Truth

When you're researching the history of the Negro Leagues, it's virtually impossible to avoid the legend of James "Cool Papa" Bell. Considered possibly the fastest man ever to play professional baseball, Bell was one of the marquee players in the 1920s and '30s. The tomes written about the Negro Leagues are full of stories about Bell's speed. Bell would frequently score from second on a routine fly ball; one time, he even stole two bases on a single pitch. His 175 stolen bases in 1933 for the Pittsburgh Crawfords is one of the great, untouchable records. (To be fair, it was a season with between 180 and 200 games, but the MLB record isn't even close—138, set by Hugh Nicol in 1887.) Bell was elected to the baseball Hall of Fame in 1974 and, in 1999, was ranked 66th on the *Sporting News* list of the greatest players in history—one of only five players on that list who played all or most of their career in the Negro Leagues.

As I got deeper into my work of locating and contacting

former Negro League players, however, I heard a story about Bell that shook me up. Bell, who was eighty-seven when he died in 1991, and worked as a janitor at the St. Louis City Hall for many years after retiring from baseball, would open his arms to people who wanted to come by and talk to him. Sadly, it was common knowledge among Negro League aficionados that there were some awful people who unforgivably exploited Bell in the last decades of his life as a result of his friendly demeanor. There were guys who would come to his home in St. Louis, make him sign hundreds of items, give him $20 for his time—and then maybe take some of his original memorabilia with them when they left, for good measure.

This culminated in 1990, when two men were put on trial for stealing hundreds of thousands of dollars' worth of items from him. Here is how columnist William Rhoden described the case in August 1990 in the *New York Times*:

Last April, a dealer was indicted on charges of stealing $300,000 worth of photographs, bats, balls, posters, pennants and uniforms that Bell had collected in his 30-year career. According to Bell's daughter, Connie Brooks, who eventually discovered that the items were missing, the men came looking for autographs from Bell. Then over a four-day period they came back, she said, and while one occupied Bell and his 83-year-old wife, the other carried out boxes of relics. Bell has testified that he and his wife felt "trapped" and feared that they would be hurt if they attempted to stop the men.

Bell wasn't the only one exploited by collectors—I heard stories of other former Negro Leaguers who were also mistreated and not fairly compensated. Many players weren't aware of the explosion that was taking place in the sports memorabilia market in the 1970s and '80s, and had no idea that the items stashed in their closet, which they had long been told were worthless, could actually, suddenly, fetch big money. These stories were especially upsetting as I came to better understand the financial circumstances of many former Negro League players. I began to really get why guys like Wayne Stivers and Gary Crawford would make sure I sent money whenever I requested a player's autograph. They were trying to protect these players—many of whom had spent a lifetime being promised things that they never received. At age thirteen, I wasn't an expert on the long American history of economically exploiting Black men. But I sensed that if a legendary Hall of Famer like Cool Papa Bell had to work as a courthouse janitor to support himself, there was something wrong with the picture.

Even if former players weren't being directly exploited, as Bell and others had been, many were still just barely scraping by financially. This point was hammered home when I came across an obituary for a former player who had died at the age of ninety-eight and had worked shining shoes up until the very end of his life. I probably had about $50 to my name in the bank at the time, but I had the safety net of my family. I began to recognize that many of the former players I was reaching out to didn't have that, and that signing an autograph for a thirteen-year-old kid, no matter how excited that kid was to talk to them, was probably pretty low down on their list of worries. I had recently tried calling an eighty-year-old former player before finding out his phone had been shut off because he couldn't pay the bill—something I'd never had to worry about. I was beginning to wrap my head around the painful realities of the American economy, and how too many of these guys I was starting to care so much about were likely to be on the outside, looking in.

I was also starting to get spooked by how often I would search and search to locate a player—only to get back the letter I'd sent out, returned to sender with a depressing word written on the front: *Deceased.* The finality of it all would weigh on me. Once they're gone, they're gone. I decided at that point that if I needed to stay up another hour to make a couple more phone calls or send a few more emails, that's what I had to do. I knew the clock was ticking, and the thought that if I didn't act fast enough, another player might be lost to history, started to drive me more and more.

This is when Bob Mitchell entered my life. Perhaps more than anyone else, Mitchell, a former Negro League player himself, made me understand the unfortunate circumstances many former players were in. Mitchell was a right-handed pitcher who was signed by Buck O'Neil to join a pitching staff that included Satchel Paige. He played for the Kansas City Monarchs for four seasons, from 1954 to 1957.

My first email to Mitchell, who lived in Florida, was sent on August 12, 2008. It read:

hi mr mitchell,

i was wondering if i could send you a few items to have signed
> *im 13 years old and am a huge fan of the negro league.*
> *thanks you very much,*

cam perron

My communication skills obviously needed some work. I rarely used spell-check, did not structure my messages, and clearly didn't capitalize. A little bit of background information on myself probably would have been helpful. Mr. Mitchell, who I would come to learn didn't hesitate to tell you what he thought, got me in check with his response a day or so later.

Cameron Perron,

I/we don't normally give out autographs, etc. via requests by mail nor from telephone calls. There are professional collectors out there that benefit from the rarity of any form of memorabilia of/from the few living legends of the Negro baseball leagues. Of course some of us make visits to schools where we gladly sign autographs. . . .
> *I've had collectors query me for certain legends' photos, etc. I've been serving as the National Coordinator of the Communication Network of Negro Leagues Players for the past eight years to present, and as I've acquired several*

pensions for dozens of former Negro League Players with many more in whom I'm seeking some form of compensation for players who did not meet the criteria of MLB, you caught me in a fairly good mood this A.M. And I DO NOT GIVE OUT MY TELEPHONE NUMBER, it should be obvious to avoid being harassed by collectors or non-sense calls. (813) 247-XXXX, today after 1:30 P.M.

Bob "Peach-head" Mitchell, Sr.

Mitchell's response was both generous and educational. I was glad to be making a new connection with a former player as well connected as Mitchell, and as devoted to improving the lives of Negro Leaguers. But there was also something buried in his email that caught my attention—mention of the Major League Baseball pension program for former Negro League players.

Mitchell and I started talking to each other on the phone, and during one of those conversations, he told me that he had secured a pension for a player named Clyde Golden. Apparently, Golden got an initial check from MLB for $60,000. I was stunned. I started to do some research into what the deal was with these pensions. I learned that, in 1997, Major League Baseball had announced that it would give pensions to Negro Leaguers who had been confined to Black teams before 1947—the year Robinson broke the color line—and had also played for at least four years. Largely through Mitchell's forceful lobbying efforts, MLB then amended the policy in

2004 to include players who had been on Black teams into the late 1950s, since MLB didn't fully integrate until the Boston Red Sox added a Black player in 1959. Even after 1959, most teams continued to operate with informal policies to only have one or two Black players at a time.

The May 15, 2004, edition of the *Washington Post* reported the story of Mitchell's successful lobbying efforts under the headline: "MLB Agrees to Make Payments to Negro League Players":

> A group of former players who met the four-year requirement but didn't start their careers until after 1947 has agitated for some sort of compensation since the creation of the original plan, arguing they were denied a full opportunity to play in the 1950s and thus qualify for a Major League pension. The effort attracted [Florida Senator Bill] Nelson's support in 2001 and gained momentum on March 10 of this year, when [MLB commissioner Bud] Selig pledged to deliver an initial proposal to Nelson's office within a month.
>
> [Bob] Mitchell, himself a former player, said he spoke with nearly all the 27 players yesterday and received their support for Major League Baseball's latest proposal.
>
> "Under the circumstances, I'll say it like this; the strife is over, the battle is done," said Mitchell, 71. "Based on the length of the time I've been doing this, the expenses out of my pocket from doing this, I've

been feeling a little stressed. It's good that we're getting to the climax of this thing. I'm very happy for the guys to be able to realize this, because it was a long struggle on my part, and it was a lot of patience on their part, waiting with hope for this to happen. Now it looks like it's going to happen, and I just praise the Lord for it.

I also learned that when the original pension program was announced by MLB in 1997, they had put a former player named Joe Black in charge of administering it. Black had played for the Baltimore Elite Giants for seven years in the 1940s, then became the first Black player to get credited with the official win in a World Series game, in 1952, as a pitcher for the Brooklyn Dodgers. After the Dodgers, he went on to pitch for the Cincinnati Redlegs and the Washington Senators.

At the time of the 1997 announcement, Black was asked to put together the list of players who would qualify for the pension. Though he was familiar with many Negro League players, there was a limit to how many he knew about and could vouch for, and many players who were eligible for the pension got left off the list. That's where Mitchell came in. Once he got the rules changed to allow for players who had their careers on Black teams in the late 1940s and in the 1950s to get pensions, he started contacting MLB to advocate for specific players who weren't on Black's original list. He actually forwarded me some of the emails he had sent to MLB. I got the impression that he had become became a persistent gadfly, calling MLB offices nearly every day to advocate for Negro League players. I'm sure he annoyed league executives, but he was a godsend to the players who had been denied playing opportunities because of racism and were now being spurned once again.

MLB responded to Mitchell's appeals, but at some point the efforts started to go bad when a few of the players applying for pensions were caught fabricating their histories. Reportedly, one player created a contract that was obviously fake: he had whited out multiple lines on a contract he had found online, and edited it with a modern-day font that was typed on a computer, not a 1950s typewriter. Another player Photoshopped his face onto an old photo. As a result, MLB backed off a bit, making it harder for players to make a case and instituting more stringent requirements of proof. Players now needed to have hard evidence that they had played in the Negro Leagues for at least four years, meaning one item of primary source documentation for each of those four years. These could be newspaper articles, dated photographs, official scorecards, programs, or a verified playing contract. For most of these guys, in their seventies and eighties, that kind of documentation was almost impossible to gather.

While I found the pension information that Bob Mitchell keyed me into intriguing, I didn't see how it was immediately relevant to me or how I could help with it at the time, so I set it aside. What occupied most of my attention at this point was the business of making my own baseball cards for the Negro Leaguers I was getting to know.

The idea had come from Gary Crawford, the Negro League researcher and aficionado who had called my house asking for my mom after I bought an autographed photo from him on eBay. I had started to have frequent conversations with Gary. He worked in sports marketing and broadcasting in Chicago and had become interested in the plight of former Negro League players after he met a few of them in the Chicago area. He tried to brainstorm ways he could help them make money, since many of them seemed to be in poor finances. He would bring players to baseball card shows, where they would sign and sell photos and perhaps make a hundred bucks or so. Although there were limited numbers of players on publicly available lists, Gary and I knew there had to be many, many more players out there who were still alive but had never been located. It was uncharted territory.

Gary knew I was only thirteen, but he seemed to appreciate having someone to talk to who shared his interest. And besides, Gary liked to talk. A lot. We came up with the idea for me to create baseball cards for the players from scratch. I could send the cards to the players, and they could then make a few extra dollars by selling them to their friends and family, members of their church, or people who contacted them about their careers. Better yet, they would have an additional item to sell at any card shows that might pay them to do signings.

Unfortunately, we didn't have much initial luck with the card shows in the Boston area. We reached out to the organizer of one show, seeing if he had any desire to bring in a couple of Negro League players. We were told that there wasn't enough interest in the Negro Leagues to justify paying former players to come to a show. My social consciousness was increasing at this time, and I saw that this might be a predictable part of Boston's shameful history with race. After all, Boston was the last city to integrate its baseball team and had typically trailed behind most other cities in its willingness over the years to hire Black athletes. I was upset that this guy would pay $10,000 for a Boston Red Sox benchwarmer to attend a card show, but couldn't spare $200 to bring in a Negro Leaguer. It felt to me like history repeating itself.

Regardless, the card idea still seemed promising and appealing to the players I mentioned it to. I started with Bill Bethea—an incredibly kind player who had become my frequent pen pal. Bethea's Greensboro Red Birds were a semi-pro all-Black team that played against most of the top Negro League teams when they came through the South. He also briefly joined the Raleigh Tigers of the Negro Leagues for a handful of games. Bethea was such a good pitcher that he still holds the record for the lowest ERA in a season (1.25) in the South Atlantic League and the most strikeouts in an extra-inning game (25). He laughingly noted that he pitched for thirteen innings and didn't get the win. Bethea played on minor-league teams for the Braves, Pirates, and Blue Jays but never made it to the big leagues—though many who saw him pitch professed that he certainly was good enough.

In the letters we'd been trading back and forth, he let me know how tough things could be financially. He was diabetic and had medical expenses to keep up with. It wasn't much, but I figured if he could sell twenty cards for $5 each, he could make a hundred bucks, which was better than nothing.

July 14, 2008

Hello "Cam,"

How happy I was to hear from you and to hear that you and your family are well. . . .

I regret to say that most of my teammates have died. There are a few left, but I don't hear from them very often, but pray that they are still among us and are in very good health at this time. . . .

My computer has stopped working at this time, but I hope to have it checked out very soon. Bills and taxes plus auto repairs have limited my spending as I am on a fixed monthly income. Things will get better, I pray.

Until next time my "little inspiration." Keep it together.

Sincerely,
Bill Bethea

My mom is an artist, so I used her Adobe Illustrator account to create a card design that I thought would work, using a picture of Bethea from his playing days. Bob Mitchell helped me decide which paper stock to use. He went to Staples and determined that 120-pound card stock would be the best approximation of a real baseball card. I sent my early designs to Mitchell and he critiqued them, suggesting small adjustments to make.

I made about twenty of these original cards for Bethea, and when I sent them to him, he loved them so much that he asked for two hundred more. In one letter about the cards, he told me: "I've received so many compliments about them. I

Negro League Baseball

Bill Bethea Pitcher

My first homemade baseball card, for Bill Bethea (made in 2008, from a photo of Bethea playing for the Greensboro Red Birds in 1954).

really can't thank you enough for doing this for me—you feel so much like family (son) to me, and I love you for it."

Bill was one of my favorite people in the world, but two hundred cards was a daunting number. Making twenty seemed to take forever—I didn't have a paper cutter, so I'd used scissors to cut up each sheet. However, the message was clear: more cards were required. Bob Mitchell had thought highly of them as well, and started sending me pictures of himself and other players, requesting that I make cards for all of them. I had to figure something out.

So I looked around and found a company based in California called Custom Sports Cards that made specialized trading cards: for example, parents would use them to make cards for their children who were in Little League. The pricing was a bit steep, so I emailed the guy who ran the company and told him that I was just a kid, and I was trying to help a former Negro League player make baseball cards to sell to his friends.

The guy at the company in California was sympathetic and quoted me the wholesale price for the cards. They looked a lot better than the ones that had come off the family printer, and they only cost me about 18 cents each. I was in business. Even with the discount, I was operating at a loss, but my whole purpose in making the cards was to try to help the players, so I didn't mind. As the number of requests for cards increased, however, Bob Mitchell started sending me emails insisting that I charge the players money for the cards.

COMEBACK SEASON

Cam:

*Now ANY cards that you make for players, I want you to
REQUEST a fee of a minimum of $10.00 for the purpose of
covering any return postage to a player for any cards that
you make. . . .*

*Make it known to the player that I strongly endorse
they give you the fee before any card is made from the
photo they send to you, along with a $10.00 money order
(lest they chance cash!). I think that the players will benefit
by having baseball cards made by you, to keep their historical Negro League experiences alive. I thank you for the
recent cards you sent me. I desire many more cards. . . .*

*Remember, NO FEE from the players, NO CARDS . . .
they can afford your efforts.*

Your Legend, Bob "Peach-head" Mitchell, Sr.

It didn't feel right to me to charge the players, and I wasn't
so sure they could afford it. But one of the former players that
Mitchell sent my way, Irvin Castille, loved the cards so much
that he insisted on sending me money anyway, at times as
much as $100. For some reason I didn't understand, Castille
also preferred the homemade cards I did myself to the ones
from the professional company.

When I looked Castille up, I saw that he was a shortstop
and third baseman who'd played for the Birmingham Black

Barons from 1951 to 1953. He was good enough to have been selected for the East-West All-Star Game in 1953. When MLB held the special draft of surviving Negro League players in June 2008, Castille was drafted by the Oakland Athletics. A week later, he'd also been honored by the San Diego Padres. Castille now lived in Los Angeles, California, and he'd done well for himself financially. Because of his newfound notoriety after the special draft, I suppose Castille was getting a lot more requests for his autograph. My cards probably were coming in handy.

Castille and I started to talk on the phone regularly and send letters back and forth. He was an incredibly gracious person, and always made me feel good about myself. He was also so enthusiastic about our conversations that he requested I send him a signed photograph of myself for him to display. Now we were trading signed photographs of each other.

Aug. 19, 2008

Hi Cam,

Thank you very much for the cards. I like them a lot.

Got your package today, August 19, 2008. I was overwhelmed at the professional cards you designed for me. Tell your mother and father, I am very proud of the talented and thoughtful young man called Cam, my little 13-year-old friend. They have a very levelheaded son.

I have seven grandchildren: four boys and three girls.

*One graduated from college and one will attend Arizona
State. I hope you will continue your education.*

*Enclosed are three signed Cam cards and $20. I have
adopted your signature suggestions.*

> *Your friend,*
> *Irvin Castille*

This type of connection only fueled my desire to locate and
contact more players. At the end of 2008, I was able to significantly step up my ability to do exactly that. I had just turned
fourteen. I succeeded in convincing my mother to sign me up
for a paid account on a site called Net Detective, a research
tool that provided unlisted phone numbers. I used the money
I made from odd jobs to pay her back. With that new access
to information, I developed a fairly sophisticated system for
tracking down players. I would get a roster for a Negro League
team, like the 1963 Kansas City Monarchs. Sometimes, the rosters would denote a player's age—though I soon learned not
to trust it, as players were known to fib to make themselves
appear younger. So the technique I had more luck with would
be scanning the list and picking out the players with the most
unusual names. Those are the ones I would target first. When
I got a return hit from Net Detective of a list of people with
that name, I would use my growing knowledge about the cities and regions where former players were more likely to live
to rank and narrow down my priorities. I was much more
likely to get a hit with the names that were in or near urban

centers like Chicago, Detroit, Memphis, Birmingham, and Atlanta. Sometimes the rosters would list a hometown where the player was from, and over time I noticed that most of the players I was contacting still lived near the places where they had grown up and played ball. Even if they had moved away at some point, most often, they eventually came back home.

When I saw the name M.C. Johnson on the Monarchs roster, it didn't take long for me to find him on Net Detective, living in Chicago. Fifteen minutes later, I was talking to him on the phone. It was safe to say there weren't many individuals with the name M.C. in the United States. Thirty minutes later he had given me the name and number of a former teammate who lived close by. Just like that, I had found two more guys.

I sent Wayne Stivers daily email updates:

"Hey Wayne, I found four more guys today!"

"Wayne, I got five more today!"

Wayne began to give me assignments to find players for him, providing me with just a name and a state or city. Once I found them, Wayne would call them and interview them for the historical record. By February 2009, I had reunited half of the 1963 Kansas City Monarchs. My skills were being honed to the point where I felt like I could find anybody, anywhere.

CHAPTER 6

Going Pro

I'd now located and made personal connections with dozens of former Negro League players, so I started to look for other researchers who were as passionate about the Negro Leagues as I was and might be interested in hearing what I'd been up to. Perhaps, I thought, by sharing information—as I had done with Wayne Stivers, Gary Crawford, and Bob Mitchell—other researchers and I could assist one another in finding more players, increasing our opportunities to help those players out and deepening the historical record of the Negro Leagues.

I knew that in most years since 1998, a gathering of Negro League aficionados called the Jerry Malloy Conference had taken place. Malloy had been a well-known baseball historian, and the conference brought together Negro League fans, collectors, and historians to discuss and promote Black baseball history. I looked into the upcoming event and saw that it was going to be in Pittsburgh. Asking my parents to drive me nine hours to get there seemed unreasonable. However, I saw that it was possible to submit a paper to the conference without attending, which if accepted, would get into the conference's publication. That sounded perfect—the more I'd looked into it, the more boring actually going to the conference had seemed, since there were barely any former players who went. It was mostly older researchers giving presentations.

I decided I would write a paper on Bill Bethea. We'd been friends for more than a year at this point, and I felt deeply connected to Bill. I had dozens of long, handwritten letters from him, had made him baseball cards, and he'd educated me extensively on the history of his career. I was proud when the researchers in charge of the conference accepted my paper and published it, giving me my first byline. Looking back, I can't help but cringe at some aspects of the style and substance of my writing at the age of fourteen. But while it may not be a literary accomplishment, I think the paper illustrates the steady expansion of my consciousness of the disadvantages, racism, and unfair treatment Bill and so many of my new friends had really experienced in their lives. It also shows how Bill responded to that treatment—with unbelievably hard work, a stoic attitude, and a drive to prove doubters wrong. Finally, it shows just how excited I was that players like Bill were willing to share their incredible stories with me, and let me share those stories with others.

Here's what I wrote in that paper:

Bill Bethea was born on August 21, 1929 in North Carolina. He grew up around Greensboro in a house with no running water or electricity. His family had to go to a nearby well to get water, had to use a wood stove to cook, and needed to go outside to an outhouse to go to the bathroom. There were also no paved roads where his family lived. He was raised mostly by his grandparents but learned many things growing up, and was taught to love and respect everyone.

As a teenager Bill was known for his basketball skills, everyone knew "Billy Bethea" who was one of the top players around the Greensboro, NC area. He played basketball at the Windsor Recreational Center which was the only recreational facility for African American children. Later on Bill played basketball and went to school for two years at Dudley High School, in Dudley NC. This school was an all-Black school and was not yet integrated when he went there. After a three-year break of no school, Bill enrolled in a private high school called Immanuel Lutheran College where he continued to play basketball. Later on he also played in the Rucker's Tournament, and was the MVP of the Rucker's League. Bill's most memorable moment was being asked to play basketball for NYU, but he couldn't because he had already signed a professional baseball contract.

One day the Greensboro Black Yankees were playing at a field close to where Bill lived (they were an all-Black local team). The team was short a player for the three games they had scheduled, so they begged for Bill to come and play with them, and so he did. The first game with them he played outfield, and he had a few balls hit to him. The balls he threw back would always "tail" and would never go straight in. This excited the manager and he realized Bill would make a good pitcher. This scared Bill and made him not want to play if he had to pitch; he had never played baseball before but had played some softball. Bill ended up pitching anyway and struck out an astounding 21 batters which most professional pitchers do not even do!! This amazing performance really drew attention to Bill. The third game that was scheduled was supposed to be played against the Greensboro Red Birds. Unfortunately they were unable to play that game. The next time the teams met, Bill's uncle saw him (his uncle was on the Red Birds). He was asked to come play with them, and he accepted.

Throughout the year of 1954 Bill played with the Greensboro Red Birds. The Red Birds were a semipro Negro League team. Bill taught himself to become a very good pitcher with an average of over 15 strikeouts per game, he was a strikeout machine. He also developed his own "Knuckle Curve Ball" which really fooled batters. The Red Birds "barnstormed" (toured the country playing baseball) and played against many high class players and teams. They would ride a bus from game to game, and eat canned food on the bus because they could not go into many restaurants. These players were not allowed to play in the majors because they were not white, so they formed their own teams and leagues. They were just as good, if not better than the major league players and probably could have played in the majors. They had to work twice as hard to succeed, and were paid a lot less than white players. This all took place because "the time was not right." Racism still existed and prevented African Americans from getting as far.

Bill did not know it, but while with the Red Birds a man named Gil English had been scouting him. Gil had played in the majors with many teams throughout the 1930s (he passed away in 1996). Gil soon signed Bill to play for a Boston Braves farm team called the Wellsville Braves. This was the start of Bill Bethea's extraordinary minor league career. Pay was a lot better in the minors, and the other players' skills helped Bill improve. Bill went on to pitch for teams like the Clinton Pirates (played with Sweet Lou Johnson), St. Jean Canadians, Raleigh Capitals (managed by Enos Slaughter), and with the Lexington Indians. Bill also went to spring training in Florida in the late 50s and pitched against Larry Doby and Luke Easter (look up their stats).

When Bill Bethea joined the Lexington Indians, he and another teammate became the first two Blacks to play on the team. They had to deal with lots of racism and negative remarks but they managed to integrate the Lexington Indians. Fans shouted at him and called

him "the n word" and "Satchel Paige" in very embarrassing and insulting ways. He was not allowed to stay
in hotels like other teammates, so he stayed in people's
houses. One time a riot started because fans did not
want Bill to pitch. Bill pulled up his shirt and showed
the angry fans that he had an Indians jersey on and
had the right to play. Bill tried not to let these types of
things effect him. He decided to win them over rather
than be mean about it, and that ended up working. Bill
Bethea finished his baseball career with the Lexington
Indians in the early 1960s.

Bill Bethea played 6 years in the minor league and
also played with the Greensboro Red Birds in the
Negro Leagues. He worked very hard and worked his
way up to the class B level, but fell shy of making it
to the "show." Unfortunately he injured his arm and
that halted his career. He always tried to work harder
than everyone else. While with the Lexington Indians
he would warm up by running 30 laps, while the other
players would run 10 or 20. Bill always tried to remain
in "tip-top" shape and do his best. On June 17, 1996 Bill
Bethea was inducted into the South Atlantic League
Hall of Fame for his amazing career as a pitcher.

When the Malloy Conference publication with my paper
in it came out, I looked through and kept coming across the
name Dr. Layton Revel. It was a name I'd heard mentioned
before by Wayne, who told me Dr. Revel was a top-notch re-

searcher who had located many Negro League players over the years. I sent Dr. Revel a couple of emails over the course of the next few months but didn't get a response. In the spring of 2009, I finally reached him on the phone. It was an eye-opening conversation.

Dr. Revel was a fifty-nine-year-old white doctor who lived in Texas, working to rehabilitate patients who had suffered medical malpractice or had long-term medical conditions. He was as passionate and committed to the Negro Leagues as I was, but he'd been doing it a lot longer than me and had a different set of resources. He'd been locating players since the 1980s, researching the Negro Leagues and building up an incredible archive of contacts and interview transcripts—not to mention a trove of Negro League artifacts, uniforms, programs, all sorts of items. He hoped to house these one day in a new Negro League museum, for the posterity of future generations.

The more I talked to Dr. Revel, the more I realized that we approached our shared goal of connecting with former Negro Leaguers, with the same mentality, though with vastly different tools. Dr. Revel told me that in the early days, after he'd contacted a player he would fly to whatever city he lived in to meet him. That player would typically then connect him to other players, and he'd meet as many as a couple dozen guys over the course of a week. By the end of the trip, Dr. Revel would host a dinner or barbecue and invite all the players he had met. He would spend hours interviewing them and collecting autographs that he could use for his future museum.

He repeated the same process in cities all over the U.S. Since I had yet to meet face-to-face with any of the players I'd contacted, I was amazed at his technique, old-school and analog as it was, and a little bit envious of his stories.

As it turned out, Dr. Revel was a little bit envious of me as well. He didn't even really use email, as I'd discovered when trying to contact him. He had an email address but rarely checked it. When I explained to him how I used Net Detective to find players all across the country by typing their name into a search engine and then combining research and common sense to cross out all the men with that name until I had located the player I was looking for, his mind was thoroughly blown. He was from the generation of "411"—the telephone information line—which he often called, keeping operators busy for hours and racking up hundreds of dollars in charges in the hope of finding and connecting with a player. While he was calling every Willie Smith in the entire state of Alabama, I was narrowing down my list to the right guy, all from behind my computer screen.

Dr. Revel and I started working together. He would give me leads for players he had been clued in about and wanted to find, and off I would go, usually tracking them down quickly using my internet tools. We were getting such benefit from the relationship that we began talking on the phone nearly every day. Despite a forty-five-year age difference, we soon became very close friends.

I'll let Dr. Revel explain our relationship in his own words:

To understand my relationship with Cam, it's important to go back to the beginning of how this all started for me. In the late 1990s I attended a reunion at the Negro League Museum in Kansas City. I was a big collector and had long been interested in the Negro Leagues. There were 258 former players they had brought to the reunion. Buck O'Neil was there, and I had met him before, so I asked him, "Buck, how many players did you guys have to invite to get 258 players here?"

"You know, Dr. Revel, you got to realize there's less than 275 players alive," he told me.

My son and I went around and got everybody to autograph a baseball for us. I looked around at the exhibit and asked the director, "This is a nice exhibit, but where are all the bats, the balls, the gloves, the trophies, the uniforms? Where are all the historical artifacts?"

"Well, Layton, none of that stuff survived," he said.

I didn't think very much about it. When I got home, I was looking at a list of the players I met. There was a guy on there, Tony Lloyd, who played for the Birmingham Black Barons in 1960. I thought about his age and realized that there had to be more players out there. Then I carried it one step further and thought about the artifacts. I had known Satchel Paige, who died in 1982. I knew Buck Leonard—in fact, when Buck had a stroke, his wife called me and asked if I could talk to Buck's doctor to help him get a rehab program into place that would get him back to being able to sign autographs. I had known Cool Papa Bell; I had been in his house in St. Louis multiple times. I knew that all these players had artifacts. I owned autographed balls from all of them, in addition to a number of other artifacts, like original photographs. Things I had picked up here and there over the years. I didn't feel it was a true statement that there were no artifacts out there.

I decided to investigate further, so I flew up to the museum again in Kansas City to discuss it with them. I told them I'd like to see their archives because I wanted to do some research.

"Oh, Dr. Revel, we don't have any archives," they told me.

"Well, every museum I've ever known or been associated with has archives," I said. "How do you store all your historical documentation?"

They told me they didn't do any of that. I responded that I would set up a research institute there and fund it myself.

"I'll put an endowment in place where we can buy historical artifacts as they come on the market, or if players and families want to sell things," I said.

They told me that while that was a very generous offer, it's not what they were looking to do.

"Obviously you're going to commit a lot of money to this," they said. "We would appreciate you just giving us that money in the form of a donation."

Hmm, no, it really doesn't work that way, I thought.

I was getting frustrated. Next I flew to New York and went up to Cooperstown, to the National Baseball Hall of Fame. Surely, I would get a more enthusiastic reception at America's home of baseball history.

"Layton, you've known us a long time," they told me. "We barely have money to pay our bills. We kind of go from one induction ceremony to the next. History is important, but we got the whole history of baseball."

Bottom line, they couldn't or wouldn't do anything.

I headed down to New York City to meet with Major League Baseball and the Players Association. MLB said that's not what they were focused on at the time. The Players Association said, "Layton, if it doesn't put money in the players' pockets, we're not interested."

My efforts fell on deaf ears everywhere I went. When I got back home, I was very disappointed. I was complaining about it to my family when we were sitting at the dinner table.

"Dad, you know a lot of people around the country," my son said. "Why don't you do something about it?"

The proverbial lightbulb flipped on. I proceeded to set up a 501(c)(3) nonprofit foundation called the Center for Negro League Baseball Research. We have no paid employees. All of our associates work on projects, spending money out of their own pockets. Our primary activity is trying to find ballplayers and artifacts.

I came by my interest in the Negro Leagues first as an athlete myself. I grew up in a small town in Louisiana and played everything in high school—football, basketball, track. I played basketball in college, I played on the All–Air Force basketball team; I played a year of semipro basketball in Dallas. I had a tryout with the San Antonio Spurs, but it didn't last very *long. I was the first player that got cut. I'm only five feet, eleven and a half inches tall—though I had good bounce and could dunk a basketball. But I didn't have the ball-handling skills of a Marques Haynes or James Silas or Oscar Robertson. College basketball and semipro basketball was kind of the highest level I could go. So I started collecting.*

When I started collecting, I got to meet a lot of players. The thing that impressed me about all the Negro League players I met was their attitude of not feeling sorry for themselves, not feeling like they were taken advantage of, not feeling that they've been screwed because they couldn't play in the major league. I think there was so much professionalism there. And these guys played for the love of the game of baseball.

The two things I really focused on were, number one, the fact that it's a piece of history that has been forgotten. Secondly, when you talk to the ballplayers, you could not find a more gracious group of individuals. The players were just happy somebody recognized that what they had done a long time ago was very important. We had not done really anything in the United States to document and preserve the history of Black baseball. That's what got me started.

It was a labor of love years before I met Cam. I networked regularly with about fifty people around the country who were very serious about Negro League baseball: Wayne Stivers in Denver, who just enjoyed finding players, getting autographed baseballs; Larry Lester, who is in my consideration the premier historian on Negro League baseball in the country, and the author of several books. We developed a network of professionals doing research and preserving and collecting the history. What was interesting to me was that nobody was making any money off of it. Nobody gets paid. When I do a TV or radio show, I get asked all the time, "Well, Dr. Revel, how do you make money at that Negro League baseball stuff?" The answer is we've never made any money. It costs a tremendous amount of money every year to run this thing. I financed the operation of the Center for Negro League Baseball Research myself; we've done a lot of really good work.

One night I get a phone call from a young kid in middle school named Cam, who said he had an interest in Negro League baseball and asked if I had any players he could talk to. Impressively, he had already contacted a number of players on his own, and was looking to reach more. I had a ready group of about eight to ten players I leaned on in these situations, so I gave their information to the kid, knowing they'd be kind and professional. Cam called everybody on the list and was back on my phone a few weeks later, looking for additional players. I gave him more names. A few weeks later he was back, seeking more. This went on for a few months. I was intrigued that a young white kid from Boston was interested in the Negro Leagues; I was impressed by his persistence. As I talked to Cam more, it became clear to me that this kid had a skill set on the computer and the internet that I did not possess. After a year or so of us talking fairly regularly, I began to give him assignments, sending him out to look for players that nobody had ever tracked down. I was pleased when Cam started finding a bunch of them. It confirmed my suspicions that there were still a lot of living players out there. It really aggravated the dickens out of me when people would tell me they were gone, the history was gone with them, and there was nothing anyone could do about it. I felt that people had taken that position because finding these players would take too much work. You couldn't go on the internet and type "former Negro League ballplayer" and get a list of names of players that hadn't been found yet. You couldn't go on eBay. You had to do research. You might have to dig through the archives of old Black newspapers like the Afro-American *out of Baltimore. It would take work; a lot of people aren't interested in work. I would get phone calls all the time, somebody asking me, "I'm writing a story, can you give me the lowdown on how Jackie Robinson broke into major-league baseball?" Or somebody just died and they called me so that I can do all the work for them when they are writing the obit. It's kind of like gold mining. You go into an area and you look around. If you don't see big old nuggets of gold laying on the ground, you might conclude there's no gold there. It's not easy, but if you know what you're doing and are willing to work, you might find gold there. That's what it's like looking for Negro League players.*

After a year of my working with Dr. Revel, we had tracked down and interviewed about seventy-five players that nobody had ever talked to before on record! It was an exhilarating time.

Dr. Revel had also taken a major interest in the pension

Dr. Layton Revel *(right)* with Lawrence "Fats" Nelson in New Orleans, 1999. (Nelson caught Satchel Paige's pitching debut in the Negro Leagues for the Chattanooga White Sox in 1926.)

program, and let me know that he was working with players to secure the proof that they needed to show MLB that they had been active in the Negro Leagues for a minimum of four years. I thought this was interesting, but I was so busy locating and contacting players that I still didn't think much about the pensions at the time. I was at the point where I was juggling active relationships with forty to fifty former players, talking to each of them at least once a week. Whereas I had previously been on the phone for an hour or two, a couple times a week, now I was on the phone for four to five hours a day, every day of the week. My head and neck would hurt by the end of the evening from holding the phone against my face. It was nuts. Players would call my house while I was in school, and my mom would have to tell them that I wasn't there because it was 1 p.m. on a Tuesday. I always told them I was a teenager and that I went to school, but I think some eighty-year-olds had a hard time remembering the logistics of a fourteen-year-old's life.

Often a player would call during school and say something to my mom like: "Just tell him the baseball player called." I don't think they understood how many other players I was talking to. My mom quickly recognized it was key to write down the player's name and number, or else I'd have to sift through the phone call history to backtrack and find who it might have been, which took a while when I was calling so many numbers a day.

Thankfully, my mom enjoyed talking to the players, too. "They were genuine and nice and friendly," she says. "It wasn't like when Cam was young and we went to get autographs from Red Sox players, when they looked at you funny and didn't seem to want to be doing the signing even though they were getting paid a fortune. These former Negro Leaguers were just so nice. They'd call the house and some of them used to go on for hours talking to me, telling stories. They just loved to talk. A lot of them were Southerners. They were more respectful, they had manners. And they didn't care what Cam's age was. They never asked about his race. They didn't ask about my race. It was never an issue at all."

My mom is right about the lack of focus on race.

Some of the players I was talking to knew that I was white; others didn't seem to know, or wonder about it at all. It wasn't something that they typically brought up during our conversations. When they did, they never seemed to dwell on it. I suppose that for the players who did know, my race might have made my interest in their lives more intriguing to them, but that wasn't apparent to me when we talked. It always seemed to me that the fact that I was white, and these guys I was spending so much time getting to know were Black, was of more interest—and, for anyone who disapproved, concern—for outsiders looking in, than it ever was for me and the players.

CHAPTER 7

The Birmingham Gamble

Toward the end of 2009, after so many hours getting to know former Negro League players on the phone, I finally got the chance to meet one of these legends in person. His name was Jim "Mudcat" Grant. He had been a star player in the major league for teams including the Minnesota Twins, which is what most people know about him. In 1965, while playing for the Twins, he became the first Black pitcher to win twenty games in a season for an American League team. That same year, he became the first Black pitcher to win a World Series game for the American League (he actually won two complete World Series games for the Twins in the 1965 series, and hit a three-run homer in Game 6). That season, Grant was the *Sporting News* American League Pitcher of the Year. But what most people didn't know was that before his sterling major-league career, Grant played a season with the Negro Leagues' Raleigh Tigers. This was a fact that was left out of the biographies I found of him on the internet.

Since 2008, I'd had a little side job helping out Phil Chiaramonte at his monthly Vintage Sports Promotions memorabilia show at the Hilton Garden Inn in Burlington, a few towns over from Arlington. Phil had even let me set up a memorabilia table of my own at one of the shows, though that had turned out to be a big waste of time, as I'd sat there for hours waiting for customers and barely made any money. Instead, I mainly assisted Phil, doing whatever odd jobs he needed. He paid me about $50 per show.

When I told Phil about the work I'd been doing with Negro Leaguers, he surprised me by saying he also had an interest in the Negro Leagues. He had been doing the show for a couple of decades at this point, and he told me he'd brought in some Negro Leaguers in the late 1990s and early 2000s. He said he'd be happy to bring a former player to the memorabilia show again for a card signing event—assuming the player lived close enough that the travel expenses, which Phil would cover, would be reasonable. I got very excited about the idea, until I realized that out of all of the players I'd located and contacted up until that point, not a single one lived nearby.

I kept the notion of bringing a player to Phil's show in the back of my mind, though. And in the fall of 2009, I found out from Gary Crawford that he had made a connection with Mudcat Grant and brought him to Chicago for a memorabilia show there. Gary suggested that Phil and I could likely get Mudcat to come to Boston, which I thought was a great idea. It was a perfect suggestion because Mudcat's playing legacy went beyond the Negro Leagues into a thirteen-year major-league career for seven different teams, meaning there would be plenty of regular fan interest in him, even in Boston. As I've mentioned, Boston was not a place these guys typically visited, for understandable reasons.

When I approached Phil, he gave it a thumbs-up. The only problem was that Mudcat lived in Los Angeles. So I put on my agenting hat and became a fourteen-year-old broker—the Doogie Howser of agents. I spoke with Gary about Mudcat's fee, and even researched cheap flights to get him from L.A. to Boston.

"What the hell is AirTran?" Gary asked when I told him about the inexpensive flight I had found.

It's now defunct, but in 2009 it was alive and well, and we booked Mudcat a flight on the airline. In addition to covering the travel, Phil agreed to pay Mudcat about a thousand dollars for his appearance at the upcoming October memorabilia show.

I was elated that it was actually going to happen. For the month before the appearance, I bought all the Mudcat Grant cards I could find, planning to get them signed. I was more than a little obsessed. I thought this was so much cooler than meeting the Red Sox and Boston Bruins players I'd waited hours in line to say a few words to.

When the day finally arrived, October 10, 2009, and Mudcat came to Boston, he didn't disappoint. A driver that Phil had hired picked Mudcat up at the airport, and Mudcat stayed at the Hilton Garden Inn where the show took place. Mudcat wound up getting a solid turnout of sixty-five to seventy people, who paid a few dollars to get into the show, and then $15 to have one of their items autographed by Mudcat, or $25 for two items. In addition, Mudcat agreed to autograph two to three hundred items, such as baseballs and photos, that Phil could continue to sell after Mudcat was gone. Phil wound up making a small amount of money on the event, which meant it was a success; you didn't go into memorabilia and card shows to become the next Jeff Bezos.

I was glad the event was a financial success, but the real thrill came from spending time with Mudcat. The memorabilia show had two rooms—the autograph room and the

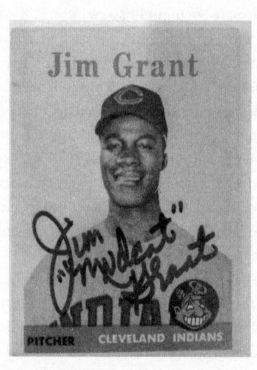

My 1958 Topps signed rookie card of Jim "Mudcat" Grant playing for the Cleveland Indians.

dealer hall—and my job was to man the autograph room, stamp the attendees' tickets as "paid" when they came in, and then facilitate the interactions between them and Mudcat, making sure he signed the item where the person wanted it. What this meant was that I got to spend the entire day with Mudcat. In between signings, we talked about baseball, life, music—all sorts of things—which seemed refreshing to him after so many people just wanted to ask him about the greatest game he played in. He was a gracious, friendly guy, and I felt honored to get to know him a little bit.

The experience with Mudcat also made me realize how much better it was to get to meet players in person than to only talk to them on the phone, or by letter or email. The opportunity for connection was that much greater in person, and stories could come out that just might not do so otherwise.

It made me seriously think about Birmingham for the first time. Through conversations with Dr. Revel, it had become clear that Birmingham, Alabama, was pretty much the center of Negro League baseball. Many of the guys who had played with teams in the South, like the Birmingham Black Barons, had stayed in that area after they retired from traveling around in the leagues. They got jobs at the many steel mills and factories that were thriving in the Birmingham area at the time, and many continued to play high-level baseball for company-run teams, in what was known as the Industrial League. Some of those teams were really good. These players got married, had kids, and made a life there. Decades later, Birmingham still had a cohesive unit of former Negro League players who kept in touch with one another—a community of players that no other city in America had. They would sometimes get together for events, to speak at schools, and to talk about the Negro Leagues. If I could find a way down there, I might be able to meet a lot of players in one trip.

Dr. Revel had a good friend in Birmingham whom he worked closely with on Negro League research. The friend was a well-respected local celebrity chef named Clayton Sherrod, known to everyone as Chef Clayton. Clayton was the first Alabamian inducted into the American Academy of Chefs—aka the Hall of Fame of chefs. Long before that, he had been a batboy for the Black Barons in the late 1950s as a ten- to twelve-year-old. Clayton remained obsessed with the Negro Leagues from that time forward. Clayton was also friends with many former Negro Leaguers in the Birmingham area.

Chef Clayton and Dr. Revel were talking together one day and realized that the one hundredth anniversary of Rickwood Field was coming up in June 2010. Rickwood Field, the oldest ballpark in America, was the first home of the Black Barons and had hosted many of the biggest baseball stars in America—Black and white—over the years.

Dr. Revel came to me with an incredible idea: What if we invited all the players we had gotten in touch with to Birmingham for a big multiday reunion event that coincided with a celebration of Rickwood Field?

That's all I needed to hear—I was in. While Dr. Revel and Chef began all the logistical planning, I got to work inviting the players.

Dr. Revel and Chef Clayton had held a smaller reunion banquet the year before at the Sheraton in Birmingham and had lost quite a bit of money because the turnout was disappointing. I could tell they were nervous about that happening again. They were placing their hopes on my ability to wrangle a crowd of players to Birmingham. The existing group of known players who lived in and around Birmingham were pretty sure bets to join, but to make it work we needed to get the larger group of players I'd recently found, who lived around the country, to show up as well.

Looking back, I can see that I clearly should have sent out formal invitations in writing, but I didn't know any better, so I gave the players phone calls explaining the agenda for the trip, telling them we'd be taking care of their hotel rooms, and asking if they'd come. Dr. Revel and Chef Clayton were fundraising to cover expenses and also putting in some of their own money, so the players wouldn't have to pay for anything besides their travel.

Every time I got a yes from another player, I passed the name along to Dr. Revel with pride. He was a bit skeptical about the strength of the commitment, though, knowing how easily life can get in the way of the best-laid plans.

"They said they're coming—why wouldn't they come?" I told him. "They said they're all packed for the trip and they've told their former teammates they're going to be there."

But I could tell he was still uncertain about the verbal commitments. To Dr. Revel, until a player walked on June 1 into the lobby of the Redmont Hotel—which would be our home base for the reunion, where we and all of the players traveling from out of town would be staying—it was only speculation.

One player in particular, named Charlie Dees, put me through my paces just to get his verbal yes.

Charlie Dees had appeared in ninety-eight major-league games over the course of three seasons (1963–65) for the California Angels (they changed their name to the Anaheim Angels in 1997 and then the L.A. Angels in 2016). But before his MLB career, he played with the Louisville Clippers of the Negro Leagues in 1954.

I'd first contacted Charlie long before I was inviting players to the reunion. His name had been put on a list of the most difficult "gets" for autograph collectors—guys that no one had been able to crack over the years, making their autographs that much more valuable. There was a 1964 Topps set that included one of his cards. Many collectors of vintage signed cards had gotten the majority of their other cards in that set signed but couldn't get Charlie's. It was especially intriguing because, while his address was well known, collectors regularly tried to reach him and reported getting no reply. I knew that collectors would pay well over $100 for Charlie Dees's autographed card. Of course, it was my nature to be drawn to the challenge.

I decided on a bold plan of action: I would call his house on Thanksgiving. I figured it was the day when he would be likeliest to answer the phone, when family members would be calling to wish him a Happy Thanksgiving. I was a little nervous since I had heard he might not be the friendliest of players, but I figured, *What do I have to lose? I've been hung up on hundreds of times, and called out-of-service numbers hundreds of times more. How much worse could this be?*

When I called, Dees answered the phone right away. *It worked!*

I began to go into my spiel about wanting his autograph, and when Dees had heard enough, he cut me off and said, "It's fifty dollars an autograph. Whitey Ford charges fifty dollars; I charge fifty dollars."

I thought to myself, *Whoa, Charlie, Whitey Ford is in the Hall of Fame—you are no Whitey Ford.*

But instead of challenging him on the fee, I took a different line of approach.

"Is it true you played in the Negro Leagues?" I asked.

I started dropping names, telling him about all of his former teammates I had talked to—even from some of the minor-league teams he had played on. I could tell he was starting to soften his stance. I told him I could send him a bunch of his own cards for his own use, guessing that he probably didn't have a big supply. I also told him I would send him phone numbers of his former teammates, in case he wanted to reach out to them. By the end of the call, I had talked Charlie down from $50 to $30 per autograph. When I hung up, I ran into the living room and let out a yell, startling my parents.

I sent Dees three cards to sign, along with $90, and I put up a notice on the SportsCollectors.Net site, letting people know about my big get. When I got the signed cards back from Dees, I sold one of them to a collector for $150. I kept getting messages from more collectors, asking if I could help them obtain Charlie's autograph for their collections.

I'll admit, my relationship with Charlie had started with some crass commercialism and the excitement of doing something others hadn't been able to, but Charlie and I soon became friends. He was one of the guys I would check in with regularly to chat. He was happy that I had put him in touch with old teammates, with whom he enjoyed talking about the old days.

When I first told Charlie about the reunion and asked if he would come, he said no. Charlie never really left his house in Atlanta. His favorite thing was to be at home with his wife watching shows like *Judge Joe Brown*, *People's Court*, and *Judge Judy*, which he told me they would do from 11 a.m. to 5 p.m., every day. But I knew what would get his attention. At his heart, Charlie was a businessman—he had worked in the record business for many years after retiring from baseball, and owned record shops, among other things—and he was always open to hearing about new ways to make money.

"Charlie, if you go to the reunion, I'll see if I can work out another autograph signing," I told him. "I can guarantee you five hundred bucks."

"Really?" he said.

"And you'll get a free hotel room in Birmingham."

Birmingham was only a two-hour drive from Atlanta.

Charlie had grown up there, and still knew many people in the area.

"Okay," he finally said.

With Charlie and many others now having said yes, I had more than fifty guys who'd told me they would be coming to the reunion. I *had* to go. But there was a problem standing in my way—the bane of most, if not every, kid. School was still in session.

I was fifteen years old at this time, and into my sophomore year of high school.

I didn't think it was a big deal to take a few days off. Honestly, I had come to consider school to be kind of a joke. *What does it matter if I miss a week learning about Christopher Columbus?* I thought. Kids should be encouraged to take time off to pursue passions—and what better example than this?

Luckily for me, once again, I had parents who understood. My mom got wind of what was going on and wanted to help. So, to get me to Birmingham, Alabama, she broke into my room and stole some of my stuff.

I'll let her explain:

When Cam was in high school, he hadn't done much traveling up to that point. Even when he played sports, the teams didn't do any of those trips where you travel somewhere far away and have to stay overnight. It was mostly local stuff. So, when this reunion in Birmingham came up, and Layton Revel really wanted Cam to go down there to help him out, I knew that my husband and I had to figure it out. We agreed that I would go with him. But then we realized the reunion was during school. It wasn't a vacation week or a weekend or anything. He was fifteen and a sophomore in high school. It's an important time to be in class. Missing almost a week was a lot. Still, we knew that the reunion was important, too, and we had to figure something out.

I went up to Cam's room when he wasn't home and read the letters from Bill Bethea. I had looked through them briefly before, but I had never really read them. Bethea talks in the letters about how people would be throwing tomatoes at him and his teammates on the bus, and how they even had to spend the night on the bus at times because they weren't allowed in hotels or motels in certain places.

They were such painful, yet beautiful letters. I read through all of them and I was blown away. I realized, wow, this is historical. This is a big deal. I made an appointment to meet with the guidance counselor, to get Cam excused so that he wouldn't get in any trouble for missing school. Cam didn't know about it. I brought the books and the letters to show her. She couldn't get over it, how impressive it all was. She immediately was like, "Yes! Go!" So the school gave him permission.

Eventually the whole school knew about it. The dean talked to him. They all thought it was a pretty cool thing. It was a big moment because, while Cam was a good student, he wasn't taking honors or AP classes that would propel him to the top of the class. He wasn't great at sports, so he wasn't going to get any sports scholarships. At this point in high school we started thinking, You know what? He's got these skills that are really cool. *But we didn't know how to easily explain what his skills were. Most college scholarships are academic. The type of thing he was doing was unique. So it was good to have the school supporting us.*

My husband said, "You know, for Cam this is kind of like a business trip. He's fifteen, but this is his business." That's exactly what it was! That was a cool moment, when we realized that. We knew it was important to him; this is what he does. We never knew where the skills were going to take him. Our friends used to ask us, "What is he gonna do with these skills?" We would honestly have to tell them, "We don't know, Cam could become a historian. He could be a reporter. He could be a writer. He could be a collector." We didn't really know. But we liked the fact that he was doing something that was entrepreneurial. My husband and I both had our own businesses then—I had a product-licensing business creating office supplies and giveaways with company logos on them, and then transitioned into running "paint and sip" classes for people interested in having a good time and a glass of wine while learning to paint. We get what it is to be entrepreneurial. It's something that we encouraged.

When my mom told me that she had gone into my room without my permission and stolen rare and valuable artifacts out of my closet, I was a little pissed at first, but I soon started to see it as funny and a real gift. She'd gotten the thumbs-up from the school. It was really happening. We were going to the reunion!

Before we left for Birmingham, I got the following letter from Dr. Revel, outlining his expectations for what I would be doing there. It sounded so official and important. He sent similar, personalized letters to all of the players and other attendees. My excitement, already high, smashed through the roof.

05-10-10

Dear Cam,

I am pleased to invite you to be part of our research team for our Birmingham, Alabama, research trip on June 1–4. The events that we will be covering and help sponsoring during this research trip will be as follows: the 100th Anniversary Celebration of Rickwood Field; Southern League and Negro League Players Reunions; Negro League Reception at the Alabama Sports Hall of Fame; and the Alabama Negro League Players Association and Museum of Negro League and Southern League Baseball History Sports Banquet.

The focal point of the trip is celebrating the 100th anniversary of Rickwood Field which as you know was the home of the Birmingham Barons (Southern League) and Birmingham Black Barons (Negro American League). Rickwood is the oldest professional baseball park in the

United States and this is the first time that both white and Black players who shared a stadium have been brought together to recognize their baseball accomplishments.

I anticipate that we should have 10–15 Southern League players and as many as 30 Negro League players attending the events. Harmon Killebrew (Member of National Baseball Hall of Fame and former Chattanooga player) will be one of the special guests.

Your specific assignments during this research trip will be helping with the players' portrait sessions, oral histories interviews, and hosting the ball players. In addition, I would like you to meet with Dr. Linda Revel [Layton's wife] and Dr. Debra Horne as they are developing an educational program on researching Negro League baseball that will be used in public schools. Your research in Negro League baseball has been exemplary and you will prove to be an invaluable resource to their work. I especially want you to share your research techniques with Dr. Revel and Dr. Horne. This program is something that next year will be taken to the Birmingham area public school systems. It is also a program that could be used in your local school system back home.

This trip represents a once in a lifetime opportunity in Negro League baseball research. We look forward to you and your family being a part of it. Your participation in this event will help preserve the history of Negro League baseball in America. The educational experiences that you receive during this project should be very valuable to your *high school experience and will undoubtedly look very good on your college applications.*

Please call me if you or family has any questions.

Sincerely,
Dr. Layton Revel

For the entire week before we left, I was on the phone every available minute, confirming that everybody who told me they were going to be there was still in. I spent the little bit of extra time I had helping Dr. Revel out with something to do with the pension program—my first time really assisting in that area. He was working with a player named Paul Jones to secure a pension. Dr. Revel had documentary proof that Jones had played in the Negro Leagues for three years, but he needed to find a record of a fourth year, and they were having trouble doing so. Using internet newspaper archives, I scoured through hundreds of articles before finally coming across a box score from a game in 1948 when Jones pitched for the Homestead Grays. It was the missing year, and Jones's name was right there, in digitized ink. I printed it out, tucked it into my suitcase, and planned to show it to Dr. Revel in Birmingham.

After we took off from Boston, we had a layover in Charlotte. While we were at the Charlotte airport, I got a call from Gary Crawford, who told me he had just read an article about a blind ninety-two-year-old former Negro League player named Roosevelt Jackson, who lived in Georgia. While sitting there at the boarding gate, I tracked down a number for Roosevelt Jackson and gave him a call.

"Hi, Roosevelt, my name is Cam," I said when he answered the phone. "I'm a Negro League baseball researcher, and I'm actually on my way to a Negro League reunion right now."

"Oh yeah? When does it start?" he asked.

"It starts tomorrow," I said.

"What's the address?"

"You gotta go to the Redmont Hotel in Birmingham, Alabama," I said.

"All right," he said. "I'll get on the next Greyhound bus."

I hung up the phone, amazed and a little incredulous. And then I had a moment of doubt. I swallowed hard and thought—maybe Dr. Revel was right about those verbal commitments. Could I really count on the players I'd invited to show up?

CHAPTER 8

Family Reunion

When my mom and I arrived in Birmingham and walked outside of the airport terminal, my first thought was: *Whoa! It's hot as hell.* Coming from Boston, where summer comes on slowly, I wasn't prepared for the nearly ninety-degree June heat in Alabama. Then a white rental van, with the words "Anthony Underwood Motors" on the side, pulled up, and out of it stepped an older gentleman with a white beard. It was my buddy Dr. Revel, in person before me for the first time. We shook hands, and he patted me on the back. I know how glad I was to see him, and I got the sense he was happy, too. He told me that he and Chef Clayton had raised over $10,000 to put on the event, and all the pieces were finalized. The van had come from an arrangement Chef Clayton had made with a local auto dealer, and there were a few more on loan to transport the players around Birmingham. We were ready to go.

I caught up with Dr. Revel as he drove me and my mom through downtown Birmingham. The buildings were beautiful—a type of classic Southern architecture I wasn't familiar with at all—though the city streets seemed quiet to me compared to the hustle and bustle of Boston, and I was a little surprised by how few people I saw. At a stoplight, I took the newspaper article out of my bag that proved Paul Jones had played in the Negro Leagues for a fourth season, and handed it to Dr. Revel. He was grateful and excited, but there was so much going on that we quickly moved on to another topic.

My mouth fell open as we pulled up to the Redmont Hotel. It was elegant, and tall, with two stories of white terra-cotta topped by eleven more of light brown brick. Between the first two floors was a flag-draped balcony that jutted out over the sidewalk. Dr. Revel told me the hotel had first opened in 1925 and was the oldest in Birmingham still in operation.

When I walked into the lobby, I was overwhelmed. Beneath the vaulted ceilings and massive chandelier was a room *full* of former Negro League players who had recently arrived at the hotel and were checking in. They were clustered in groups, chatting and laughing, soaking in the joy of one another's company. I'd invested hundreds of hours over the course of nearly a year along with Dr. Revel and Chef Clayton trying to get them to Birmingham, and here they were: they'd really come. It was incredible. Dr. Revel's wife, Linda—who is a doctor as well—was there with a couple of her church friends, greeting players when they walked in, checking them in and handing them their name tags, which had been prewritten. The hospitality was amazing—there were a bunch of volunteers helping the players, handing out water, getting them something to drink from a little bar area that was set up. Food was on its way. I couldn't believe how much planning the Revels and Chef Clayton had done.

I wasn't sure where to start. I knew the life stories of almost every man in that lobby—sometimes I knew details that even their families hadn't heard—but I had no idea what anyone looked like. All of our conversations had been on the phone, or by letter and email. There weren't many pictures of these guys on the internet. And for the players I'd made baseball cards for, the pictures I was using were from more than half a century earlier. So I took a moment to hang back and just soak it all in. Then, slowly, with my mom's encouragement, I wandered up to the guys and began to introduce myself.

To my amusement, some of them reacted with surprise. I was not the version of Cam they'd been expecting. When I approached Charlie Dees, he actually seemed confused. I gathered from the way he reacted that he hadn't known I was white. It was a bit awkward for a moment, but as soon as he made the connection, we bonded like old friends.

For most of the other players, their response to meeting me in person was summed up with the phrase: "I thought you were going to be a little nerd with glasses!"

They thought of me as being glued to a computer, researching history. That was true, but I didn't look the part. Instead, I was wearing jeans and a Red Hot Chili Peppers T-shirt: my typical outfit of the time. I had messy hair, and no glasses. I was tall, lanky, and held myself pretty confidently. Oh—and even though I'd faked my voice on the phone to make it sound deeper when I'd first started calling players two years earlier, by this time, my voice had gotten legitimately deep on its own.

As soon as the players got over my appearance and recognized who I was, they welcomed me with open arms. They were so used to the way I talked and the way I thought; the only thing that had been missing was the way I looked. It felt like being reunited with a group of old friends that I'd been close with for a long time. The same was even more true for the players, who were reconnecting with one another after fifty or sixty years apart.

They jumped back into their friendships like no time had passed at all. Everyone had so much energy. As the day went on, more and more players arrived. Reginald Howard drove from Memphis, and he brought Bill Little, who had played on the Memphis Red Sox and the Kansas City Monarchs. Jaycee Casselberry, who played on the Indianapolis Clowns, pulled up in his brand-new Mercedes SUV and walked in with a thirty-pack of Budweiser. That was his thing—he said he always brought Budweisers with him because his son worked for Budweiser, and he had a house full of them. The players started telling tall tales, messing with one another, drinking a couple of beers. Jaycee told everyone that Russell "Crazy Legs" Patterson, his good friend and former roommate from the Indianapolis Clowns, had stolen his girlfriend Theresa back in 1960. Jaycee started yelling "Theresa!" and causing a scene. We couldn't stop laughing; it was all in good fun. It was impossible not to feel the love in that room.

At some point around midnight, an old man walked into

the lobby, with a woman who looked to be in her late twenties. It turned out it was Roosevelt Jackson, the blind, ninety-two-year-old former player, with his granddaughter. I introduced myself and helped them check into their room. I couldn't believe it—they'd actually gotten on a Greyhound bus and traveled from Georgia, just as Roosevelt had said he would when I'd reached him on the phone earlier in the day. It was the first time a reunion like this had happened, and he wasn't going to miss it for anything, short notice be damned.

By the end of the night, about forty players had arrived and been checked into the hotel. I was so exhilarated, there

Me with Roosevelt Jackson at the Redmont Hotel during the first Birmingham Negro League Players Reunion, June 2010.

were so many people to meet and stories to hear, I didn't go to bed until 1:30 a.m.

The next morning, a lot of the players who lived locally in the Birmingham area joined us. I had talked to many of them on the phone before, but with the ones I hadn't, the other players vouched for me.

"Oh, that's Cam," they said. "He's the researcher guy I told you about."

With the local players included, we now had around a hundred people total in our party. We sat for breakfast together, which was the first time I ever tried grits. I didn't like them, but everyone said I needed to eat them at a place that really knew how to make them.

Dr. Revel made a speech at the breakfast, welcoming everyone who'd recently arrived and laying out the agenda for the day. After breakfast we'd be headed to the Rickwood Classic, which, this year, was doubling as a celebration of the hundredth anniversary of Rickwood Field. Before the game, the Negro Leaguers would go on the field and be acknowledged in front of the crowd.

Rickwood Field is the oldest baseball stadium that's still in use in the world. It was built in 1910 to be the home of the (white) Birmingham Barons, and holds more than ten thousand fans. Babe Ruth often played there with the Yankees, as did many other big stars. When the Birmingham Black Barons were founded in 1920 and joined Rube Foster's Negro National League, Rickwood became the Black Barons' home field, too. They would alternate schedules with the white Bar-

The Birmingham Black Barons at Rickwood Field, late 1940s.

ons based on who was playing out of town. Black Barons players Satchel Paige and Willie Mays dazzled fans there. Jackie
Robinson and Hank Aaron later did, too. Rickwood remained
the Black Barons' home field until they disbanded in 1963.

Though they eventually moved to a new home field in the
mid-1980s, the white Barons (who of course had long since
been integrated by that point) continued on as a minor-league
team through a few different iterations. Since 1986, they've
been the AA team for the Chicago White Sox. Every year, they
return to Rickwood Field, from their current home stadium in
the Birmingham suburb of Hoover, and take on another AA
team for the fan-favorite Rickwood Classic event. At the Classic, the two teams wear throwback uniforms, and the stadium
sells programs for a nickel. The umpires wear white shirts
and bow ties.

Back at the Redmont Hotel, the players were excited and
wanted to look good for the event, too. A few of them were

wearing replica versions of their own original jerseys. These were the few players who had been to events celebrating the Negro Leagues in the past, and remained the most actively involved in keeping the legacy of their playing days alive. Most of the guys, however, didn't have anything like that. They'd never been to an event celebrating their careers, of any kind. But here was their chance: some of the savvier players had come prepared, and were selling Negro League gear out of their trunks. Carl Long, who had played for the Black Barons and in the Pittsburgh Pirates farm system, sold shirts and hats out of his big pickup truck. The players started pulling out their wallets, clustering around Carl's truck, trying on items and stocking up on gear. Russell Patterson probably spent $300, getting a jersey and a multitude of hats, pins, and buttons. By the time we headed over to Rickwood, at the very least all the players had throwback hats displaying their former teams.

I could feel the palpable sense of history as we walked up to the stadium. It's painted bright green, with all-caps lettering spelling out "RICKWOOD FIELD" and a red-tile roof. Fans were starting to gather, though they didn't seem to take much notice of us at first. As we entered the stadium, I was wowed once again. The field had been preserved brilliantly, with a re-created manual scoreboard that required volunteers to scale a thirty-foot ladder and stand on scaffolding to change the score each time a base runner crossed the plate. The lights dated back to 1936. The outfield wall was covered in 1940s-styled advertisements for companies like Pepsi-Cola, U.S. Steel, and the local Tutwiler Hotel. Baseball movies like *Cobb*, *Soul of the Game*, and more recently *42*, have used Rickwood as a filming location.

In 2010 the Barons were hosting the Tennessee Smokies—the Chicago Cubs' AA affiliate—and before the game started, the former Negro League players attending our reunion would get a few moments in front of the steadily building crowd. My task was to line them all up in a particular order and make sure that their names and former teams were written down properly, so that the PA announcer could call them out individually on the field. We had many players in wheelchairs, and others with walkers, so it took a good twenty minutes to get everyone organized. Then, one by one, they slowly made their way onto the field. My buddy Frank Evans—who had played for a number of Negro League teams, including the Black Barons, and had gone on to coach in the St. Louis Cardinals organization—was one of the players in a wheelchair, and I pushed him onto the field. (Not so easy when you're on grass.)

Each player had his name read out, and I moved over to stand outside of the foul line, wearing a press pass, taking photographs. When players' names were called, they mostly took off their caps and bowed. Players like Russell Patterson and even the ninety-two-year-old Roosevelt Jackson did little dances and shimmies. After the names were called, we all left the field and settled into seats by the third-base line, forming

Attendees of the first Birmingham Negro League Players Reunion at the 2010 Rickwood Classic game.

Back row, from left: Willie Lee, Otis Thornton, Eugene Scruggs, Roosevelt Jones, Charlie Dees, Joe Porter, Milton Tiddle, Willie Sheelor, Dick O'Neal, Sam Brison, Roger Brown, Carl Holden, Tony Lloyd, Earnest Harris, Henry Elmore, Bill Little, Roosevelt Jackson, Jake Sanders, Robert Underwood, Joseph Marbury.

Front row, from left: Read Blue, Jaycee Casselberry, Billy Vaughn, Willie Walker, Leroy Miller, Frank Evans, Russell Patterson, Cleophus Brown, Larry Smith, Ray Aguillard, Reginald Howard.

a little Negro League players and family area in the stands. The mayor of Birmingham, William A. Bell, threw out the first pitch, and then the game got underway.

At first, the fans in the stands gave the Negro Leaguers their space, but slowly, they began to come up and ask for autographs. It started with a few little kids. Then there were a couple of adults. By the end of the game, there was a long line to get the players' autographs and interact with them. Many of these players had gone so long without any notoriety. Russell "Crazy Legs" Patterson had been involved in baseball for many years as a coach, and often told people he had played in the Negro Leagues, but he'd come across so few people who cared. That day, he signed autographs for a straight hour. He and his old roommate Jaycee Casselberry entertained throngs of people with stories from their playing days. To have this many interested people—most of them white people, many of them kids—clamoring for their autographs, took some of the players aback. But I could tell it was deeply gratifying for them, too. It was a validation they had gone most of their lives without receiving. Now it was coming to them in abundance. As I watched it all happen, I could hear them talking already about wanting to come back in future years.

The next day, Thursday, I helped Dr. Revel conduct some official player interviews in the morning for the historical record, and assisted a photographer that Dr. Revel had brought, who worked with the Texas Rangers, to take portraits of the players wearing old baseball gloves and uniforms. I spent the rest of the afternoon hanging out with players casually. At this point it no longer felt like a gathering of friends—it felt like a big family reunion. We all seemed to genuinely like being with one another, and there was a wonderful feeling of openness and connection flowing through the group. I was unquestionably the odd one out on the face of it, a young white kid from Massachusetts, but I felt embraced and accepted. I loved it.

On Thursday night, we had a big reception at the Alabama Sports Hall of Fame. When I'd seen the itinerary for the week and the term "reception" listed next to the event, I had no idea what that meant. I didn't realize that you were supposed to wear nice clothes. And since I was fifteen, I wasn't consulting my mom on my wardrobe for the trip. So I wore baggy shorts and a double XL shirt that I'd bought from Carl Long, with all of the Negro League team logos on it, to the reception—which, as I soon learned, was attended by all sorts of Birmingham socialites and fancy folks, including the mayor. I'll admit I felt a little underdressed, but I wasn't going to let it get to me. I've always had a relaxed attitude toward clothes, and this event was about the players, not me.

What turned out to be truly embarrassing to me, however, was when Dr. Revel and Chef Clayton went up to the podium at the front of the room to give a speech. After explaining who they were and how the reunion had come together, they turned and asked me to come up to the front. They presented me with a plaque, recognizing me in front of the crowd of about two hundred people for all my efforts to track down players. Dr. Revel pointed to players like Russell Patterson and Charlie Dees, and told everyone: "Cam brought them here." I just hoped that people couldn't see my face turning red.

Dr. Revel then told the crowd the story of Paul Jones, much of which was new to me. Paul had made the trip from Ohio down to Birmingham and was in the room; I had met him and spent time with him in the previous days. I'd also brought the article proving his fourth year of playing in the Negro

Leagues, which I'd given to Dr. Revel after arriving in Birmingham. But I hadn't yet realized its impact.

"This young man . . . was able to find the newspaper article that likely will get Paul Jones his pension," Dr. Revel said. I looked to Paul and saw the gratification on his face as he absorbed what this meant. At that moment, I finally began to realize that the pension program could actually change people's lives, and I could help.

Paul Jones wound up getting an initial check from MLB for about $110,000, as well as a monthly pension check of $833.33 going forward. As of this writing, he's still receiving it.

After Dr. Revel's speech, players swarmed me, asking if I thought they might qualify for a pension. By the end of the night, I suddenly had tons of cases to investigate, and pension documentation to track down. People were asking for my email address so they could follow up with me. I was scribbling notes on index cards that were supposed to be for players' autographs. It was chaotic. It was also energizing.

The next day, my mom and I had to head back to Boston. My exciting week was over, I was sad to leave, but I felt changed in an amazing way. My connection to these Negro League players had gone from distant to extremely personal. And now I understood just how powerful the pension program could be. It was like a bonfire had been lit. I had a new mission.

CHAPTER 9

Taking On the Pensions

I now felt like the pensions could give me a real purpose that would extend far beyond my little world in Arlington. The timing was perfect, because when I got back home from Birmingham, right as I was about to reach out to Dr. Revel to catch up on all I'd missed with the pensions and tell him that I wanted to get involved on any future work, he was reaching out to me to bring me in.

I'll let Dr. Revel explain what had happened:

Years before I met Cam, Major League Baseball came to me about this whole pension issue. They told me they had put Joe Black in charge of it because he had played in both the Negro Leagues and the major league. They figured, Oh, Joe should know everybody in the country in Black baseball. That would be like somebody calling me and saying, "I understand you live in Dallas—do you know so-and-so 'cause they live in Dallas, too?" No! The MLB set up this pension plan, but they did not do the best job that they could have. They didn't do any due diligence. Joe Black gave them a list and said, "Here are all the ballplayers that qualify for pensions." So they started writing them pension checks. But then other ballplayers start cropping up, thinking, Gosh, my buddy over here got a pension check, why don't I get one?

They made several attempts to try to figure out a fair and equitable way to do this. There was no contract that obligated them to do anything. So they approached me and said, "Dr. Revel, we understand that you're one of the leading authorities on Negro League baseball in the country. You're obviously a neutral third party—a white doctor in Dallas who makes no money on any of this. When a player approaches us about a pension, number one, we want to be sure they really played, and number two, we want to be sure they really played for as long as they say they did for the teams they say they did. Could your research team take the lead on that?"

I said, "Yeah, we can do that."

"How much do you guys want to get paid?" they asked. "Do you want us to put you on retainer? What do you guys need?"

"Well, I don't need anything," I said to them. "I don't want any money. But one stipulation I'd like to make is that when we find a ballplayer that qualifies for a pension, that they get a check retroactive to when the pension plan started."

They said, "Gosh, that's easy. We can do that."

I think their feeling was that there probably weren't a lot of these guys out there. The qualifications were: guys needed to have played four years in the Negro Leagues and needed primary source documentation to show that they'd played. Not that they said they played or their buddy said they played. The MLB needed a newspaper article or a photograph that could be dated, a game program, a yearbook, something like that.

When we got the initial list of players from MLB who had approached them about pensions, they were all pretty easy to verify. There were about a dozen names. We were able to find primary source documentation for each one. The name at the top of that first list was Jessie Mitchell, who played with the Birmingham Black Barons from 1954 to 1959.

But when I got the next group of names, I saw that they were not going to be as easy. That's when I reached out to Cam.

"Cam, here's something I've got working with Major League Baseball. I'd like to see if you'd like to be a part of it. What's going to come into play here are your computer skills, your ability to go back and find newspaper articles that I'm not going to be able to find, that I don't have the skill set to be able to do."

Cam and I became partners, working with Major League Baseball to get pensions for these old ballplayers.

When we talked after the first reunion, Dr. Revel explained a few more aspects of the pension program as well. Once we had compiled the primary source documentation, the paperwork process was easy. There was an application, the majority of which Dr. Revel and I could handle. The player would just need to complete a couple of pages of basic information. As soon as MLB approved the application, players would start receiving pension money quickly.

As far as payouts went, there were two levels. The first was for players who'd played in the Negro Leagues and then made it to the major league. They would get about $2,800 a month. The second level was for the players who had played at least four years exclusively of Negro League baseball. They would get $833.33 a month, adding up to $10,000 per year. That may not sound like a whole lot of money, and it also may not be fair, but many of the Negro League players were living on minimum Social Security checks of $500 or $600 a month. For them, an additional $833.33 per month going forward was hugely impactful.

Furthermore, as he mentioned, Dr. Revel had negotiated for retroactive payments for players back to June 2004—when the pension plan had been updated to include a greater number of former Negro Leaguers, thanks to the work of Bob Mitchell and others. This meant that when a pension was approved for a player, he would get a lump sum up front of $10,000 per year for however many number of years he'd missed.

Bob Mitchell, who had done so much work to help players with their pensions, sadly had cancer and was slowing down in his efforts, so it was now up to me and Dr. Revel to spearhead the initiative.

Dr. Revel and I started by getting the lay of the land to figure out the full picture of who was receiving a pension already and who wasn't. *How could Otha Bailey not be getting a pension?* we wondered. Bailey was a star catcher for the Birmingham Black Barons for most of the 1950s, nicknamed "Li'l Catch" because of his short stature, and he still lived in Birmingham. He was a no-brainer for a pension, yet it turned out he hadn't gotten one simply because he didn't know the program existed. Joe Black, who had initially been put in charge of the pension program and created the list of players he thought would be eligible, was playing for the Brooklyn Dodgers by the early 1950s. As Dr. Revel hinted, Joe wouldn't have known a rookie like Otha Bailey, who was just starting his career in the Negro Leagues then.

We worked with Otha to collect documentation, and got him signed up for a pension. We realized there were probably a lot of other players out there like Otha who would qualify if they only knew the pension program existed. So we drew up our own list of players in this category, and got to work. Dr. Revel and I had a lot of early success on that track during our first year of working together on pensions.

For many other players, however, the situation was more complicated. If a player had only joined a team for a couple of weeks, did that count as a "season"? If their careers were piecemeal, and broken up, as was common—guys would play for a couple of years, then go back home and get a job, then perhaps start playing again for a few weeks at a time down the road—would MLB recognize those pieces as adding up to four years? The uncertainty the players had around these questions was understandable.

Roger Brown, who was president of one of the two Negro

League players associations in Birmingham, had had the type of piecemeal career that we weren't sure would qualify, but we gave it a shot. He had played, then taken breaks and spent two years in the army, then returned to the league after 1960. As it turned out, Major League Baseball told us it wasn't the fact that his career was broken up that would disqualify him, but the fact that he had played after 1960. They claimed the Negro Leagues had shut down by then. But Dr. Revel presented evidence to MLB that there was a Negro League All-Star Game until 1963, proving the leagues were in existence until that point. League officials finally gave in and agreed to give a pension to Roger Brown, as well as other players in similar circumstances.

In other cases, the problem was that aging players didn't have precise memories about the details of their careers. Over the decades, their recollections of their Negro League exploits had faded. More critically when it came to their chances of getting a pension, they didn't have documentation to guide them and prove when and for how long they had played.

This was especially understandable due to the way Negro League games were covered in newspapers, and the fast-moving schedules of Negro League baseball teams on the road. For instance, if the Kansas City Monarchs played the Memphis Red Sox on a Saturday in Memphis, the local Memphis paper might publish a story about that game in the Sunday edition. But by that time, the Monarchs might already be six hours away in Knoxville, playing another team. In Knoxville, the local paper there might only release new issues once a week, at which point the Monarchs might already be in Chicago. So the cycle would continue, and it was very likely that the players on the Monarchs never saw either article. Many of the players I talked to weren't aware of newspaper clippings mentioning their names at all. But I knew they had to exist.

As a result, digitized newspaper archives became very important in my quest to find documentation to prove the claims of former players. I used every research skill I had and dug in. It turned out that there were reports of Negro League games in a vast array of publications, from those small-town papers in places like Chillicothe, Missouri, to major Black papers like the *Chicago Defender*, to national papers like the *New York Times*.

I would make copies of all of these newspaper clippings and put them into a care package for the players. They would usually call me as soon as they got them, and I could hear the joy in their voices. Even if it was just one box score that listed their name in tiny print, they were ecstatic. If there was a picture of them, that was an enormous thrill—no matter that it was typically a grainy black-and-white image where you could barely make out their face. In many cases, it was the first picture they had ever seen of themselves in their uniform. For that reason, I didn't mind the hours it took to prepare these packages. It meant a lot to me.

After the success of the first Birmingham reunion, Dr. Revel, Chef Clayton, and I knew that we had to keep it going as an annual event. With all of the pieces in place from the first year, planning the second reunion in 2011 was easy, comparatively. Nearly all the players who had come in 2010 wanted to return, and many new ones Dr. Revel and I had recently gotten in touch with, or who had heard about it from their friends and former teammates, did, too.

My parents let me go to the second reunion on my own. It was the first time I'd ever flown somewhere by myself, and it was a freeing experience. To make things even more exciting, I was heading down to Birmingham a few days early. Chef had invited Dr. Revel and me to stay in his house—a large, newly built home with a lush and beautiful backyard, about twenty miles outside of the city, in a town called Helena. The

Chef Clayton Sherrod and Dr. Layton Revel at Rickwood Field in Birmingham, Alabama.

three of us were going on an outreach mission to meet a group of former Negro Leaguers in person in Rome, Georgia.

In one of my deep dives into newspaper archives, I had found an article describing a game in which a team I'd never heard of before called the Lindale Dragons had played the Philadelphia Stars. Lindale—a semipro team not technically in the Negro Leagues—had won, and afterward several young rookies on the team had been signed by the Philadelphia Stars. The names Butch Haynes and Bridges Jones were cited. I'd dug into the history of this Lindale Dragons team and identified several other players from old rosters, including someone named Humphrey Cole. I found Cole's number, and learned that not only was he living near Rome, Georgia, two hours from Birmingham, but Butch Haynes, Bridges Jones, and a few other former Negro League players whose names I'd come across were, too. It was a pocket of players Chef, Dr. Revel, and I hadn't previously been aware of, and while we were inviting all these guys to the second reunion in Birmingham, they were unsure if they could make it. So we decided we'd go to them.

Chef and Dr. Revel picked me up from the Birmingham airport, and we made the drive to Rome. Our destination was a big buffet restaurant off of State Highway 1 called Ryan's, where the players said they'd meet us. When we parked and went in, there were about fifteen former players already there.

It was exciting to find this big a group of players in one place. Though the food at the all-you-can-eat restaurant was gross in my opinion—bright blue Jell-O, that kind of thing—we loved getting to meet and talk to so many new guys.

I was engaged in a long conversation with Humphrey Cole, learning about his time as the manager of the Lindale Dragons, but Chef kept whispering to me and Dr. Revel: "Who's the big white guy?" There was one man, hanging out with all of the players, who not only stood out because he was about six-four, 350 pounds, but because of the light color of his skin.

We would soon learn that this was Butch Haynes, whom I'd talked to on the phone before coming, but never had seen a picture of. Butch was an imposing pitcher who'd played on the Philadelphia Stars and the Indianapolis Clowns. He'd been an all-state player with a lot of talent, but he didn't spend very much time in the leagues because the pay and working conditions were so bad.

After we talked to him, Butch decided he would come to the reunion, and I got to know him better from that point on. Butch's story was one of the most difficult, and revealing, of any that I'd heard. He had a very particular experience of playing in the Negro Leagues.

I'll let Butch explain in his own words:

I was born in Alabama, in a town between Gadsden and Centre, called Ballplay. Yes, that was the real name. I was born in the woods on April 28, 1944. My father was a white man. My mama picked cotton, and on that day he wanted her to pick cotton in the barn. So I'm a Black man with a white face.

To hear my voice, you're gonna think I'm Black, though a lot of white people think I'm a white man from New Orleans.

But I've never denied being a Black man; I never pretended to be white. My mama's Black and I'm not going to cut her short. She had to pick cotton. The least I can do is give her some credit and respect. He didn't really have to rape her. She was picking cotton for two cents a pound. He probably just got it for free like they all did. She was almost a slave—two cents a pound! And she had four kids before I was born. I never worried about that white man got my mom pregnant. Never even thought about it, so it never bothered me. I went to live with my aunt in Rome, Georgia; my mother was too poor. So I had two mothers.

I had to go to an all-Black school, which I didn't mind. I had a good life going to an all-Black school looking like a white boy. I got along with mostly everybody. White people sometimes called me "white nigger," but they called me just "nigger" more than they did "white nigger." I was treated good by the Black kids. The only time a Black guy would say something either way would be in school. One or two would call me a white boy. I didn't like to be called no white boy.

When I started playing baseball, I played for the Lindale Dragons in Rome. When the Philadelphia Stars came to town, I pitched against them and beat them. So the Stars paid me to go to Birmingham with them and pitch against the Birmingham Black Barons. I pitched nine innings and we won the game. On Monday, they wanted me to sign with them and travel. But I said, "No, you guys ain't got enough money and enough players." So I come on back. Then when I beat the Indianapolis Clowns, the Clowns asked me to join them. My *daddy came with me to the bus station and I signed a contract for $200 a month, $3 a day. This was in 1961. That night I pitched a three-hitter. In the newspaper they wrote that a white boy was on the team. I had to shave my hair a little more and I tanned good, so I got a good brown tan.*

A couple times when we went places, I was able to go into restaurants and get food for the rest of the team. I told them my father owned the factory and he wanted them to eat in here. So they would serve them.

I threw pretty hard—I was clocked one time at 101 mph. But I even had good speed on that curveball. I could throw a curveball with three balls on me. I didn't like to walk nobody. So I would tell the outfielders to get ready 'cause I was going to throw it up there where he could hit it and hope he hit it where you guys can get him out. But I didn't like to walk nobody.

I only wound up playing for five weeks. They said, "Don't go, Butch." But I said, "Man, I'm going home." The reason was I didn't like the conditions we were going through. Sleeping on that bus, not being able to get a shower. And not meeting any girls. Girls would be there, but we would have to leave before we could meet them. Anybody will tell you, I had the girls in high school. So I just didn't like it. And I don't like my meat fried hard. I don't eat hard bacon; I don't eat hard sausage. I love my food, especially breakfast. I could never get a decent breakfast because the sausage would be too hard or the bacon would be too hard. That might sound weird, but it's true.

When I got to the reunion, at first they resented me when they saw me. They thought I was white. There was a retired schoolteacher from Mobile—man, he resented me. But I understood. They've been denied the chance to play the game on account of a face like mine, and here comes a white face talking about he played some Negro League ball? Can you imagine how you would feel if you been denied and he was bragging? So I didn't get upset. I understood what they were going through. When we finally got to know each other, we had good conversations with each other.

When Butch arrived at the hotel for the reunion a few days later, an incredible thing happened that warmed people's

Butch Haynes in 1961 at age seventeen, shortly before joining the Indianapolis Clowns.

hearts. He locked eyes with Yogi Cortez, who was one of the entertainers with the Indianapolis Clowns. They'd been good friends, and hadn't seen each other since 1961. Yogi is about five feet tall on a good day. Butch, as noted, is about six-four. They embraced, shedding tears and laughing, ready to make up for lost time.

The second reunion had a lot of great moments like that. A good number of players had gotten pensions during the time between the first and second reunions, which added a celebratory feel. Lonnie Harris was one of those players who had gotten an early pension. His was an easy case—he had played eight years in the Negro Leagues, with the Black Barons and the Memphis Red Sox, and had made quite a mark. Awarded Rookie of the Year in 1953 and picked for two All-Star games in his career, Harris had played against legends such as Willie Mays and Hank Aaron and had been struck out twice by Satchel Paige.

Harris had been to the first reunion, but when he showed up to the second, he reminded everyone that he was a major character. He wore a big toupee, a fake beard, and false teeth. You kind of never knew what he was going to do next. Sometimes he'd walk into the lobby of the Redmont Hotel and demand everyone gather around and give him their attention. He would ask former players, their wives, and anyone else around how old they thought he was—and then he'd drop down to the floor and do fifty push-ups in a row. When he jumped back up, he would tell them his age, which was eighty-one as of the second reunion, in 2011.

Harris also disappeared for an entire day in the middle of the reunion, right before the Rickwood Classic event. He eventually confided in me that it was too emotionally wrenching for him to return to Rickwood, where he had once been a star. He was still heartbroken that he never got a chance to play in the major league, and felt he couldn't in good conscience go stand on the field and wave to fans and sign autographs. Having played in the Negro Leagues for the majority of the 1950s, Harris had watched others get signed to minor-league contracts, while year after year, no matter how well he played, he was overlooked. It brought home for me the fact that while many players had found some way over the years to move past the bitterness and pain about what they'd been denied, others—understandably—struggled with it still. I was glad that, although I couldn't correct any of the wrongs Harris had experienced, I could at least get MLB to hand him, in the form of a pension, a bit of financial compensation for the adversity he'd faced.

For obvious reasons, the pensions were a big topic of conversation at that second reunion. There was one player there named Frank Marsh whom I hadn't met before. I thought he could be eligible for a pension. He'd played with the Birmingham Black Barons and the Kansas City Monarchs from 1954 to 1958, and was selected to the All-Star team several times as a first baseman and outfielder. He was now a retired schoolteacher from Mobile, Alabama, and he had a reputation for being a bit rough around the edges. Marsh was the one who had given Butch Haynes a hard time when he'd first shown up at the reunion. He was openly skeptical of me and Dr. Revel. He even suggested we were profiting from our efforts—which couldn't have been further from the truth. Perhaps he was influenced by the stories of Cool Papa Bell being swindled, or just had a lifelong distrust of white people. Knowing what we knew about the things some of these players had experienced, that attitude wouldn't be unreasonable. Marsh had told us about his financial hardships. He was relying on minimum Social Security, struggled to afford basic necessities, and his phone was constantly being shut off.

Several months after the reunion, we were able to provide documentation to MLB that Marsh had played in the Negro Leagues for five seasons. He lightened up toward me and Dr. Revel quite a bit after we got him the pension, and he remained a regular at reunions after that. He would take the bus from Mobile to Birmingham, and was always one of the first players to arrive.

CHAPTER 10

Hard Work, Rewarded

Despite all of our successes with pensions, we had gotten some disappointing rejections as well. In a few cases, players I was confident would be approved had been turned down by MLB. For instance, Randolph Bowe played four seasons with the Monarchs and the Chicago American Giants in the late 1930s and early 1940s. But in his fourth year, the only documentation I could locate for him was a spring training game. In my head, I figured, clearly if he was with the team in spring training, he must have played at least one game in the regular season, but MLB said no to Bowe. Bowe was already well into his nineties at that point. It seemed to me like whatever amount of pension money MLB would have paid him for his remaining years would have been a tiny drop in their huge bucket, and that it was the least they could do to approve it. I was angry. (Bowe died in 2016 at the age of ninety-seven.)

Glemby Mosley of Staten Island, New York, was another rejection. He had played in the Negro Leagues for four years in the 1940s, with the New York Black Yankees. But in that fourth year, the team had decided to leave the Negro Leagues to travel around the country playing independently. This hadn't been Mosley's decision, and of course, he couldn't possibly know what it would mean down the line. MLB rejected Mosley's case. I found it very hard to understand their position. If a legitimate team had decided to play an independent schedule for a year or two sixty or seventy years ago, why should that be enough to keep a player today from receiving a pension?

Other cases just seemed like they came down to pure, arbitrary luck. One pitcher might happen to be written about in a newspaper article that covered a particular game, but the following day, no article was written for the next pitcher's game. So I totally empathized with the confusion and frustration of the players, who would call me regularly to check in on the status of their pensions, and to whom I would sometimes have to break tough news.

The successes, as well as the rejections, fueled my and Dr. Revel's desire to find more players who might be approved for pensions. Lodged in our minds was always the question: How many more qualifying players were out there? The search consumed us.

The case of Eugene Scruggs presented a challenge. Scruggs knew, as he told me and Dr. Revel, that he had played for three seasons that should be counted, but he wasn't sure about the fourth. In that fourth year, he suited up for the Kansas City Monarchs for just three games, when they came through his home state of Alabama. I knew his case was going to be a close call with MLB.

Eugene Scruggs was gracious enough to share the story of his career:

I was born on May 17, 1938. I grew up in Meridianville, Alabama, just outside of Hunstville. I went to a segregated school since, you know, Black people couldn't go to school with white people back then. It was a one-room school with four classes in it. All the grades were in the same room, with two teachers, Miss Kellum and Miss Snodgrass. But I didn't get a good education; there wasn't any privacy. I left when I got to the ninth grade. That's when I started playing baseball more seriously.

I was seventeen when I started playing in the Negro Leagues. I played for the Detroit Stars and then the Kansas City Monarchs. And also a local team here in Hunstville. I would go up to Detroit during the summer months and come home in the fall, around September 4. The season would start sometime in April. We would spring train and try to get players from the other teams—players who had a contract with other Negro League teams and didn't make it in the major league or something like that.

My first game with Detroit was in 1956. It was in Memphis on a Sunday in May. It was actually on my birthday, May 17. I pitched until the seventh or eighth inning, when Pedro Sierra came in to relieve me. They scored four runs off me, but I got the win—and I had nine or ten strikeouts. I was just turning eighteen, so I was younger than everybody. Some of them was old enough to be my daddy probably. But I wasn't intimidated; they were nice fellows. I was able to do what I needed to do to stay on the team.

My best pitch was the curveball. But Ed Steele, who was my mentor at the time and the team manager, would always say a fastball should be your best pitch, and you ought to be able to throw it for a strike anytime you were ready. [Edward "Stainless" Steele was an outfielder with the Birmingham Black Barons from 1942 to 1950 and also played in the Pittsburgh Pirates minor-league system in 1952.] I threw hard, probably in the eighties and maybe sometimes in the nineties. We didn't really have a radar machine, but one time someone had a radar gun and they clocked me at eighty-seven or eighty-eight miles per hour.

Though I wasn't intimidated, there were some great hitters I pitched against. Herman Green was one of them. We played on the same team for a year in Detroit, but then the next year I went over to the Kansas City Monarchs. I could knock them down with a pitch if I had to, to get them off the plate. But one day we played Detroit here in Huntsville. Herman Green hit a ball against me that went out of the park. I think it went across the street. It was a changeup. I think he was waiting on it.

It was a great moment to be around baseball back in my day. It was a cheerful moment. When our bus drove up, there would be people standing around, waiting for us. They would well-wish us into town and everything. This was what it was like before integration. Sometimes white people would come to the games. You might have a redneck come in the ballpark and holler at the players. We had one fellow that was an African-American man, but he looked like he was white when he had a cap on. A redneck was yelling about him.

"Oh, that white boy playing with these black boys?"

But when he slid into second base and his cap come off, the redneck said, "Oh, he just another one of y'all."

Eugene Scruggs playing for the Detroit Stars, circa 1957.

For nearly six years, I searched for documentary evidence to prove Eugene Scruggs's case, while many of his other teammates were already receiving pensions. Eugene would check in with me several times a month. And then, seemingly out of nowhere, an article from 1960 was digitized and added to a newspaper archive site I used. It was exactly what we needed.

I'll let Eugene and his wife Ethel describe what happened next:

Eugene Scruggs: *After waiting and trying for a long time, one day Cam called and told me that I would be getting the pension. It was such a big relief to get that news. When I received that check for $149,000, that was the most money I ever had before. The check had a whole lot of numbers in it. My wife thought it was wonderful. She couldn't believe that had happened to me. Our five kids were real happy for me, too. I have four girls and one boy; the oldest is sixty-two and the baby girl is about fifty.*

To celebrate, my wife and I booked a room at one of the nice hotels downtown [in Huntsville] and stayed for a day or two. We thought about what we would do with the money and decided to make repairs to our house here in Huntsville. Now I continue to get a check for $833 a month from the MLB pension.

I knew I had played in four seasons, but I wasn't sure about that fourth season. I had traveled with the Monarchs for a few weeks, but it was around here in Alabama. And that was that.

COMEBACK SEASON

It took a few years for them to get proof of that fourth season. It was a wonderful thing to be involved with at the time. I wouldn't trade it for nothing. I had to make some sacrifices, but it paid off in the end.

Ethel Scruggs: *I was real happy for him when I found out about the pension. We still talk about his days with the Negro Leagues. I used to travel quite a bit to see him play. But I wasn't upset when he left. I didn't mind staying home, especially when the children came.*

The money was a nice reward all these years later. I certainly welcomed it.

Eugene Scruggs: *I got married to Ethel during my third season with the Monarchs. When we had children, that's one of the reasons I stopped playing. I wanted to be home with my family as much as I possibly could. I started driving a concrete truck for a few years, then I started working downtown at the State Bank building. To make ends meet, I worked part-time at Nelms Funeral Home.*

We still enjoy going to the reunion every year. I enjoy going out to the ballpark there in Birmingham. I enjoy being there at night, when we sit around talking. I remember talking with one of the fellas, Frank Marsh, about our playing days and good times traveling on the road. One year Cam gave me a newspaper clipping talking about one of my games. I showed it to one of my grandsons and he kept it. He still has it with him.

Warriors Host Detroit Stars

Shirley Banks, Liz Shy Pace McCabe Victory

Bill Costello's McCabe Scrappers were swinging heavy bats Sunday night at O. N. Custer Park as they romped past Carver Center 25-3.

Shirley Banks and Liz Shy were the big guns for the Scrappers, each getting five hits in six trips to the plate. The game went the full seven innings.

The Scrappers play Oquawka next Sunday at O. N. Custer.

McCabe	ab	r	h	C.Center	ab	r	h
C.Shughart	5	4	3	Turner	3	1	0
J.Shughart	6	2	3	Kimbrough	1	0	0
E.Shughart	5	3	3	Cowan	3	1	0
Banks	6	4	5	Lewis	3	1	1
Krugh	5	2	0	Carpenter	3	0	0
Shy	6	2	5	Davis	4	0	1
Davis	6	2	2	Oeoherson	3	0	1
Mallin	4	4	3	Dickerson	2	0	0
Kilby	4	2	3	Bailey	3	0	0
				Goodman	0	0	0
				Tyles	2	0	0
Totals	47	25	27	Totals	25	3	4

Score by innings:
Carver Center .... 200 010 0—3
McCabes .... 006 11 11 x—25

ROVA Defeats Orion 10-0

ROVA defeated Orion 10-0 Sunday in a Warren County Hardball League game played at Oneida. Dennis Nelson went all the way for the ROVA team which was paced by Bud Wisgerhof who had three for three.

Orion	ab	r	h	ROVA	ab	r	h
Shelby	3	0	0	Wisgerhof	3	1	3
Rehn	2	0	1	Eiker	3	2	2
T.Leonard	3	0	2	Pittard	4	2	2
Crippens	3	0	1	Nelson	3	0	1
O.Leonard	3	0	0	Rednour	1	1	0
Anderson	3	0	2	Roe	2	1	0
Hamerio'h	2	0	1	Hagerty	3	0	0
Ohrberg	1	0	0	Flack	2	2	1
Lee	1	0	0	Bennett	1	2	0
Woodley	2	0	0				
Totals	24	0	7	Totals	22	10	8

Score by innings:
Orion .... 000 000—0

Jim Umbeck To Get Mound Assignment

Rain and more rain seemed to be the whole story as the Galesburg Warriors saw a 3-game weekend of baseball washed away. The Warriors will get back into action weather permitting, Tuesday night as they face the Detroit Stars in an exhibition game and then host Muscatine Wednesday in a Mississippi Valley League game.

The Stars had 95 victories and 25 losses last year as they took the Negro American League championship. Starting pitcher for the Detroit team may be Eugene Scruggs, their ace pitcher. Scruggs defeated the Kansas City Monarchs 4-2 in a recent game giving up only five hits and striking out 12 of the hard-hitting Monarchs. Coach Bucky Swise of the Warriors will be sending Jim Umbeck to the mound to face the Stars. Umbeck has been doing well this season and held the Monarchs scoreless in four innings of relief. The game will be played at H. T. Custer park and is scheduled to get under way at 8 p.m. Tuesday.

Wednesday night Doug Mills will take the mound as the Warriors face the Muscatine Red Sox in a Mississippi Valley League game. Muscatine is the only league team that has beaten the Warriors this season. Currently the Warriors stand 6-1 and lead the league. The Muscatine-Galesburg game will start at 8 p.m.

Minor Leagues

By United Press International

AMERICAN ASSOCIATION

	W.	L.	Pct.
Denver	54	31	.635
Louisville	49	41	.554
St. Paul	46	42	.523
Houston	46	44	.511
Minneapolis	43	45	.489
Charleston	40	45	.471
Dallas-Ft. Worth	37	49	.430
Indianapolis	34	52	.395

Sunday's Results
Indianapolis 5 Louisville 4 (1st)
Indianapolis 9 Louisville 1 (2nd, 7 inn.)
St. Paul 4 Houston 0 (1st)
Houston 6 St. Paul 1 (2nd, 7 inn.)
Minneapolis 8 Denver 4 (1st)
Denver 2 Minneapolis 1 (2nd)
Dallas-Ft. Worth at Charleston, ppad, rain

Saturday's Results
Dallas-Ft. Worth 6 Charleston 0 (1st, 7 inn.)
Charleston 3 Dallas-Ft. Worth 2 (2nd)
Indianapolis 4 Louisville 3
St. Paul 3 Houston 2 (10 inn.)
Denver 2 Minneapolis 1

Monday's Games
Dallas-Ft. Worth at Charleston
Indianapolis at Louisville
Houston at St. Paul
(Only games scheduled)

By The Associated Press

THREE-I LEAGUE

	W.	L.	Pct.	G.B.
Fox Cities	42	28	.600	—
Sioux City	41	33	.554	3
Des Moines	39	35	.527	5
Burlington	37	35	.514	6
Lincoln	36	39	.489	6½
Cedar Rapids	34	38	.472	9
Topeka	35	43	.346	13½
Green Bay	29	43	.303	14

Saturday
Topeka 7, Green Bay 6

The article in the *Galesburg Register-Mail* on Monday, July 11, 1960, that served as proof of the fourth year Scruggs played in the Negro Leagues, securing his pension from MLB. It reads: "Scruggs defeated the Kansas City Monarchs 4–2 in a recent game giving up only five hits and striking out 12 of the hard-hitting Monarchs."

One of the most gratifying experiences for me was the case of Joe Elliott. At the second and third reunions, in 2011 and 2012, the name Joe Elliott kept coming up. He was one of the top players in the leagues in the 1950s, a perennial All-Star for the Black Barons who could do it all on the field. Based on the records I found, he had been a standout player from 1954 to 1960. He then played a few years in the Birmingham Industrial League in the 1960s. After that, he left baseball and fell off everybody's radar. Nobody seemed to know where Elliott was or even if he was still alive. Most of the players for the Black Barons had stayed in the Birmingham area—these were the guys talking about him at the reunions—but Elliott had not. Where did he go? I wondered. A man who was once such a prominent figure in Birmingham baseball, a name that seemingly came up in almost every local baseball story or discussion: Where the hell was he?

In the third year of our Birmingham reunion, we started having more players who had played exclusively in the Birmingham Industrial League attend our events. Sometimes, a player would even just walk up off the street during one of the picnics we hosted and tell us he had played for five or six years in the Industrial League, after playing a few games with the Black Barons. In that way, our reunion was steadily growing in numbers every year with these newly attending former Industrial and Negro League players.

The Birmingham Industrial League was made up of teams assembled by some of the large industrial plants, like Stockham Steel and ACIPCO (American Cast Iron Pipe Company). It was a high-quality league, featuring many former Negro League players, as well as local star athletes who were employed full-time by these corporations. The games were big events in Birmingham's Black community. Thousands of fans would turn out to see their favorite former Birmingham Black

Barons stars play alongside top young talent at the beginning of their careers.

In 2013, a man named Calvin Holt attended our fourth reunion. Calvin was in a wheelchair; he had lost his legs due to diabetes. He had played in the Industrial League, while his brother Al Holt had played a couple of games with the Black Barons. I was chatting with him about guys he had played with in Birmingham, and once again the name of the elusive Joe Elliott came up.

"I think Elliott is alive," Calvin said. "I think he's in New England somewhere."

That was incredible news. There weren't many players in New England or anywhere in the Northeast, as I've mentioned. If Joe Elliott was living there, there was a chance I could find him, and go knock on his door if need be.

Calvin said he would try to help me track down Elliott. He called a guy who called a guy, and several months later I had a phone number. I couldn't believe it.

I dialed the number Calvin had found for me, and a man picked up who answered to the name Joe Elliott. "Hi, I'm Cam," I said. "I'm a young Negro League baseball researcher. I don't know if you realize it, but I've been looking for you for years. I help organize an annual Negro League players reunion in Birmingham, and all the former players who have attended continually seem to wonder where Joe Elliott is."

Elliott was a humble man, not a big talker, not one to brag, but I learned from him that he lived in New York City, and had worked for many years at the TKTS discount Broadway show ticket booth right in Times Square. It turns out that the man I couldn't find for years was sitting in the middle of the place that sees perhaps the heaviest foot traffic in all of America.

"I've spent years scouring through countless online phone directories with no luck," I said. "Is your real name even Joe Elliott?"

"No, it's Albert," he said. "Joe was my nickname."

"No wonder!"

And then, I hit him with the news.

"I don't want to jump the gun, but my researcher partner Dr. Revel and I are working on a Major League Baseball pension program for former Negro Leaguers. And it seems that you're pretty much automatically qualified, as you meet the criteria of having played for four years. It's highly likely you're going to get a check for a lot of damn money from MLB."

There was a long silence on the other end. Elliott had literally dropped the phone on the ground. He told me he didn't believe it. It surely sounded too good to be true, like winning the lottery with a ticket you hadn't even purchased.

"I think you could see it soon, like within a couple of weeks," I told him.

After I hung up the phone, Dr. Revel and I gathered together the evidence of his career. Elliott filled out a short form, and Dr. Revel submitted his career documentation to Major League Baseball.

As predicted, within two weeks Elliott got a check for

Joe Elliott playing for the Birmingham Black Barons, 1959.

$152,000. He was overjoyed. He valued his job at the ticket booth, and remaining busy was important to him, so he didn't quit. We were pleased when he came to the fifth annual reunion in Birmingham just a few weeks later. He arrived with his wife, Catherine, a former Olympic track-and-field athlete from the Caribbean, and his recently adopted two-year-old son. It was great to meet his family and learn more about his life outside of baseball.

As it turned out, though, the story wasn't over. I'll let Dr. Revel explain:

I was fascinated by the story of Joe Elliott. After we got him a pension, I thought it would be great if we could get Elliott to the reunion in Birmingham.

"Joe, we're having a big reunion in Birmingham and I know a lot of your friends are going to be there, like Jessie Mitchell, John Mitchell, Otha Bailey," I told him over the phone. "They'd love to see you."

"Yeah, I can come down there," he said. But he told me he had to ride on the train, because he refused to fly. Apparently, that was a major reason why he never made it onto the major-league roster for the St. Louis Cardinals, after he was signed to their farm team. You can't play major-league baseball if you refuse to fly.

After Joe arrived in Birmingham, the local Fox news affiliate asked me to come on their noonday sports show with a player, so I brought Joe with me. The host interviewed me about the reunion and our efforts to track down players, and Joe about his experiences as a player in the Negro Leagues, and getting his pension. At the end of the interview, I gave out my phone number, as I always do when I'm on television, and said to the audience at home, "If you know of any former Negro League ballplayers, if you have any information, if you have any historical artifacts or anything, call me."

I wasn't even out of the studio when my phone rang. On the other end was a lady who said she wanted to talk to Joe.

"My friend Cam is taking Joe back to the hotel right now," I told her. "Can I help you?"

"Well, I'm Joe's daughter," she said.

I'll admit, I was a bit suspicious. This had happened on multiple occasions in the past, where people came out of the woodwork when they got word that one of these old guys had gotten a windfall. It was like when somebody wins the lottery. Joe had just mentioned on television that he had gotten a check for $152,000—so here comes a woman claiming to be his daughter.

"Let me get your name and number," I said. "Let me talk to Joe when I get back. But I have a couple of questions: What year were you born in and who is your mother?"

She provided me with the answers. When I got back to the hotel, I found Joe.

"Joe, we need to sit down and talk in private," I said.

When we found an area of the hotel that was unoccupied, I said, "I thought you told me you didn't have any kids."

He nodded in agreement.

"You told me part of the reason you were so happy with getting the money from MLB is because y'all were going to adopt this little kid whose dad was in prison and whose mom was dead."

Joe said: "I never had any kids."

"Well, I talked to a lady on the phone who says she's your daughter," I told him.

He shook his head again. "No, no, that can't be."

"She was born in 1962. You were pitching for the Barons in '62." Then I gave him the name of the woman's mother.

A look of disbelief crossed his face. He went stone silent.

It turned out that the woman on the phone in fact was his daughter. When I called her back after getting the okay from Joe first, I said, "I'm going to let you talk to Joe here in a minute. But we're going to be honoring Joe and all the Negro League ballplayers at Rickwood Field. If you and your family would like to come out, your kids can see their grandfather be recognized. Joe said it was okay for us to have seats for you. How many tickets would you need?"

They came to the ceremony and met Joe. And a relationship developed between these family members. One that continues to this day.

Dr. Revel and I are now up to forty-eight successful pension stories, totaling in the millions of dollars in payouts for former Negro League players. Each one feels like a major victory. It's work that I'm grateful to be able to do, and it has created some of the most meaningful experiences in my life.

CHAPTER 11

Unexpected Attention

It never crossed my mind that the work that Dr. Revel and I were accomplishing on pensions would bring media attention to me personally. The reunion events had been covered by a few local journalists, and the players were occasionally being interviewed, which made sense to me. But I would have laughed if somebody told me to expect interest in what I was doing. In no way was I prepared for it.

It began slowly. My high school newspaper did a profile of me after I returned from the first Birmingham reunion. A few kids at the school read it, my parents were proud, but that was about it.

Then, a few months later, a reporter from the local town newspaper, the *Arlington Advocate*, got in touch with me and asked if I would do an interview for a story they were interested in running. I said yes, gave a few quotes, and didn't think much of it. But when the story ran in August 2010, I was surprised to see that it was a detailed, feature-length piece on the front page, headlined, "Arlington High School student makes his mark on Negro League Baseball." It talked about my collecting habit, the baseball cards I was making for players, and noted that I'd located and contacted about 250 players since I'd started, 75 of whom I was in touch with regularly and considered to be close friends. The reporter had interviewed Dr. Revel for the piece, and he was quoted at length talking about the work we were doing together and the six pensions we'd gotten approved for players over the previous few months. It told the story of Paul Jones getting his pension. And it included a brief quote—too short, in my opinion—from my good friend James "Cowboy" Atterbury, whom I had first gotten in touch with back in 2008 through Wayne Stivers. Cowboy and I hit it off right away, and continued to talk regularly about his career playing for the Philadelphia Stars and then Chicago Cubs minor-league affiliates.

Instead of reprinting the *Arlington Advocate* article here, which covers the things I've already described, I'd rather let Cowboy Atterbury tell his own, far more interesting and difficult story. Here's Cowboy talking about his upbringing, his ball-playing career, and some of the hardships he faced:

I was born in Cayce, South Carolina, on May 28, 1942. My mother played softball in high school, so when I was seven or eight she would pitch baseballs to us. We weren't too good, but she kept me out there playing. When I got a little older, it was different. My father played baseball in the army, but he got killed when somebody beat him up and put him on the railroad tracks when he was home on leave. I was seven at the time. They wanted people to think a train had hit him, but we found out they beat him up first. My mom didn't want me to play baseball because my dad was wild and she thought it would make me wild. Which it did. My given name is James, but when I was ten they started calling me "Cowboy" because I liked to fight.

I didn't think I was good at baseball, but I had older guys who thought I was. As small as I was, I had speed and a strong arm and I hit the ball pretty good. I was about 5'8½" and weighed about 140 pounds.

When I graduated from high school in Columbia in 1960, Pete Rose, Tony Pérez, and Johnny Bench were in Columbia playing with the Columbia Reds. They had a tryout one day, and out of the seventy or eighty kids there, they picked two of us, me and a tall pitcher. We didn't go to spring training until the following year. Bench and Rose were there. They kept me there for six weeks, but then Coach Johnny Vander Meer called me in.

"You're a good ballplayer, but you're too small for a catcher," he said. "Can you play anywhere else?"

"I can play anywhere," I said.

"Well, you go home and keep playing," he said. "You will get another chance."

I wound up playing with the Philadelphia Stars in the Negro Leagues for two years, 1962 and 1963. Ninety percent of the teams we played were white teams. They treated us fine,

*shook our hand, gave us hugs and stuff. But the spectators?
It was "nigger" this, "nigger" that. We didn't care nothing
about that; we called each other that anyway.*

*We had some trouble in Birmingham in '63. It was after
those girls got killed in that church. [The 16th Street Baptist
Church in Birmingham was bombed by members of the KKK
in 1963; four young girls were killed.] The KKK knocked on
our hotel door and wanted to see what we had in the room.
They thought we were Freedom Riders [Civil Rights activ-
ists who rode buses through the American South to protest
against segregation].*

"What are y'all doing?!" they asked us.

"We're not Freedom Riders, we're ballplayers," we said.

*It was bad, but it wasn't that bad. They didn't push us
around or anything. They didn't put their hands on us.
They wanted to see the stuff in the baseball bags. We kept
our equipment with us; I guess they thought we had guns.
They were thinking somebody was going to retaliate. But we
weren't there to mess with them. We didn't have no guns;
we didn't have nothing. They looked in the bags and saw
our gloves. They had on their white robes and their faces
covered with the masks and everything. We didn't know
what they would do, but we weren't afraid. We knew we
were there to play baseball. We weren't down there to do
any stupid stuff.*

*We were supposed to play in Birmingham, but after that
happened our manager said we need to get out of Birmingham
and get out West. So we started traveling out West. I played*

shortstop; me and this guy from Philly, Mel Robinson, were the marquee players on the team. They took care of us. I could hit, throw, run, everything. A lot of people thought I was good enough to play in the majors. They compared me to Roberto Clemente.

Buck O'Neil signed me with the Cubs organization in the 1960s, and I did play in the minor leagues for quite a while. I nearly made it onto the Cubs in '65. But I had gotten married in '62. I had kids in '62, '64, and '66. Eventually, in the early seventies, I had to get a job and take care of my family. I

James "Cowboy" Atterbury, playing for the Philadelphia Stars, 1962.

started my own business painting houses. I'm seventy-seven and still doing it. I don't want to sit around the house.

In 2011, on the heels of the *Arlington Advocate* story, I discovered I was going to be honored with an award at my town's annual Martin Luther King Jr. dinner. It was becoming apparent to me that my race was a primary reason for the interest in my story. While I could see how the place that race and racial divisions occupy in America could make the story of a white teen working with hundreds of elderly former Negro League baseball players unusual, I also found the interest in my race frustrating. The lack of coverage that Negro League players had received, the rich history of Black baseball in America, and the relationships I had built with former players were what drew me in, not race. So getting honored at the Martin Luther King Jr. event with an award recognizing contributions to racial justice and equality felt kind of wrong to me. I wasn't the only white person to get an award that day, either.

After the MLK event, the *Boston Globe* came calling. A reporter named Natalie Southwick came to the house along with a photographer—and to my mom's everlasting irritation, I refused to clean my room beforehand. Little did I realize that they would be putting their story about me on the front page of this major newspaper, complete with a rather large picture in which I was surrounded by some of my most prized Negro League memorabilia, in my messy bedroom.

The article described me as a "shaggy-haired 16-year-old

Front-page article in the May 7, 2011, issue of the *Boston Globe*.

with a shortstop's lanky build" and "one of the country's most prolific researchers into the leagues that gave Black ballplayers a professional option when they were banned from the bigs." Much like the *Arlington Advocate* piece, it recapped my journey from collector to researcher to working on the pension program. It told the story of Paul Jones getting his pension and had a nice quote from him, thanking me for what I did. It had a number of quotes from Dr. Revel. It talked about

187

the reunions. But the part I liked most was when it brought in my friend Gilbert Black, who I was in close touch with over the phone, but hadn't yet met in person.

Here's that piece of the *Boston Globe* article:

In January, he received another award at the Arlington Martin Luther King [Jr.] Day celebration. Though he is honored by the recognition, Perron said he feels rewarded simply by connecting players with one another.

"I'm just this kid that calls them up," he said. "I think it's an experience for them when I get them in touch with one of their teammates that they played with sixty years ago."

For most of those players, the human connection is priceless.

"He comes up with some things that you don't even remember," said Gilbert Black, 76, who played for the Indianapolis Clowns in 1956. "My baseball past was only a distant memory for me until Cam called me, and then it became important." . . .

"He's done me a great deed," said Black, who lives in Litchfield, Conn. "I feel very close to him, even though I've never met him. I think he's amazing."

Not long after the *Globe* article came out, Gilbert and I got to remedy the fact that we hadn't yet met in person. Gil hadn't made it to the first reunion, but he attended the second, and we had a great time together. Then, over the course of the summer and as a result of the *Globe* article, speaking requests started flying at me from all over the place. It felt weird for me to do a speaking event on my own. So I turned to my friend Gil, who was brimming with stories, and lived in Connecticut within reasonable driving distance of Boston.

The first event we did was for the Society for American Baseball Research. They had reached out to me after seeing the article, and offered me a few hundred dollars to come and speak at a meeting they were having at the Greater Boston Sports Club in downtown Boston.

Gil drove in from Connecticut and met me in Boston. It was during the summer before my senior year of high school. I still wore my usual outfit of shorts and a rock-band T-shirt. There were about seventy-five people in the crowd, mostly older white baseball researchers. They were deeply knowledge-able about league and player history, so if you mentioned any player, like, say, Mudcat Grant, they would know exactly who he was. They hadn't asked me to bring any former players with me, so when I showed up with Gil they were surprised and excited. Gil and I did a bit of planning over the phone beforehand, but for the most part we winged that first one. Gil had never done an event like this, and I had only made a few little speeches before. It was kind of like the blind leading the blind. But having Gil by my side brought me a huge measure of comfort. By myself, I would have been suffering from a serious case of what I've come to discover is called "impostor syndrome." What could I possibly say that would be of use to these old researchers? I felt much better standing alongside someone who had actually lived the history. We did okay at that first event despite the lack of planning, split the money they paid us, and decided that before the next one, we'd really get our act together.

As we did more planning and practicing, our routine came together. We did a half dozen or so events around New England over the next year.

My favorite of those events was a speech we gave at Timilty Middle School in Roxbury, Massachusetts, for their Jackie Robinson Day celebration. Ralph Branca, who was a star pitcher for the Dodgers and a teammate of Jackie Robinson, also spoke at the event. Branca, who was probably best known for surrendering the "Shot Heard 'Round the World" to the New York Giants' Bobby Thomson in 1951, was the father-in-law of Bobby Valentine, who was the manager of the Red Sox at the time.

It was a public middle school, but they must have set aside a sizeable budget for the event, because it was much fancier than the others. They put Gil up in the Fairmont Copley Plaza hotel in Boston. After checking out, Gil told me: "Cam, you should have seen the bathroom, it was the nicest I've ever seen and I didn't even spend long enough there to use it." The school administrators brought us all out to dinner the night before we were speaking. They paid Gil $500, and gave me a couple hundred as well. So I decided to actually wear pants and a nice shirt this time.

There were probably seven hundred students in the auditorium that day. Gil and I had rehearsed a version of our speech that was tailored to this younger audience. I knew the kids were likely just happy to not be in class, but that didn't mean they would have any interest in what I was saying, so as I launched into the speech, I concentrated on keeping my energy level high and making sure I wasn't putting anyone to sleep. I was only a few years removed from being the age of these students, and I felt like I might be able to really reach them.

"I know some of you out there probably get picked on for being interested in things that most kids think are weird," I said as I looked out at the crowd.

"I'll tell you right now that they're not. You should pursue those things."

I wanted to connect to all the oddballs in the audience, because I totally identified with them. I told them about how gratifying it was to help players get pensions, stressing the point that a young person did have the power to make a difference. Then Gil took over and wowed everyone. The students were spellbound as he described his career, and the prejudice he'd faced. He sprinkled his speech with lessons about American history. And he described the experience of getting the call from me out of the blue one day.

After we were done speaking, Gil spent a long time signing

four-by-six photographs that I'd printed up for him, featuring a picture of him in his Indianapolis Clowns uniform. There were so many kids who wanted to meet him.

I was in my senior year of high school when we did this event, and by then, school was something I wanted to get over with as quickly as possible. I was still a good student and managed to keep As in all my classes. But I didn't enjoy being in school.

Like most high schools, mine was divided into the typical social groups—the jocks, the nerds, the artsy kids, the drama kids, and kids like me who didn't fit into any of the groups. My interests and hobbies were considered to be strange, and I sometimes got bullied. There were guys who just didn't understand me. That was fine if they left me alone, but if somebody tried to pick on me, I'd fight back. One time in the locker room, a classmate of mine named Mitchell was being a jerk to me. I yelled back at him; he pushed me; I tried to punch him. Guys pulled us apart. On another occasion, I got up from my table in the lunchroom to get a snack, and while I was gone, a kid emptied out the contents of his tray, including meat and taco remnants and an open bottle of chocolate milk, into my backpack. It was all over my schoolbooks. I was outraged.

I grabbed the food and chocolate milk and threw it in his face. He got up and shoved me, hard. We were both taken to the dean's office, and when the dean threatened to suspend both of us, I had to speak up. The other kid wound up getting suspended, and I got off without punishment.

There were several other dumb incidents like that during my time in school—things that certainly didn't endear the place to me. These were cases of teenagers being teenagers, I knew that, but I was through with it. I had so much meaningful work in my life outside of school that I didn't have time for the silly antics of my classmates. I didn't care what they thought of me. I had fewer friends in high school as a result, but it was a price I was comfortable paying. I preferred to focus on the more important things in my life. I kept in touch with my Negro League friends, did pension research for players, and helped Dr. Revel and Chef Clayton plan the annual reunions. In addition, I had a budding memorabilia business of my own that was starting to occupy more of my energy.

The business originated when I was fourteen and began selling programs before Red Sox games at Fenway Park to make some extra money. I would stand in the middle of the sea of people flowing into the stadium and try to grab their attention: "Hey, sir, I got David Ortiz on this week's cover! Two bucks apiece—get something for the kids to look at during the game!" I did pretty well—especially with parents, who saw me as a novelty or just found me approachable—and I earned up to $175 per game. But the real draw was the increased opportunity to get current players' autographs, which I could then flip on eBay.

The autograph plan wasn't easy. I'd get to the stadium hours before the game and there would already be a mob of people with the same idea. There were a few serious autograph hounds I started running into regularly, and from them

I picked up a tip: if you have the patience and work the angles right, you'll have better luck going to the visiting team's hotel early in the day than waiting at the stadium. If you're in the right place at the right time when Derek Jeter goes out for coffee, for example, chances are high that you can get an autograph.

So, I started staking out Boston hotels, and in doing so, entered a new stage of autograph dealing. I would often find myself in a group that included some rough-looking guys outside of the hotels, but they were regular fixtures in that world of autograph seekers. My age was typically a benefit in those situations—players would come over and sign for me and a couple of other little kids, but not for the older men.

As I waited for athletes, I would sometimes see other celebrities who happened to be staying at the hotel, like musician Dave Matthews. And after doing some research, I discovered that Dave Matthews's autograph at that time was worth a lot more on eBay than a signature from the average baseball player. Unlike athletes, who knew the value of their autographs and would typically only sign one item per person, musicians also seemed happy to sign multiple items at a time.

By my senior year of high school, I'd stopped selling programs at Red Sox games and was focusing my memorabilia business almost exclusively on music. When a popular band was in town, I'd convince my mom to sign me out of school early to get over to their hotel. Steven Tyler, Peter Frampton, Sammy Hagar—I got every major rock musician that came through Boston.

I'd carved out separate places in my mind for my business in autograph dealing and my passion in researching the Negro Leagues, keeping up with players, and helping them with pensions. An interview that I did with the Boston Red Sox fan website Fenway Nation around this time hints at the way I saw my future. When they asked me whether my success as a Negro League researcher made me want to pursue that type of work as a career when I was older, I answered:

> Yes and no. I would love to do what I am doing now as a career, but there is no money in it. As Dr. Revel, a researcher in Texas I work with, has told me, it is best to establish yourself in something else, make your money there, and then do this as a hobby. I plan on majoring in business or entrepreneurship in college, but I would also love to be some sort of sports agent. Negro League players have been quickly dying off and in 15, 20 years, most of them will be gone, so I can't really do this forever, which I know. I don't think that I will ever make a career out of researching, I'm just not that type of person. Oh, and most researchers like to read and write books. I rarely read, and I don't like writing, so I do not believe I would do good with that profession.

Reading that now, I can't help but cringe at the brutal honesty and outlook of my sixteen-year-old self. *I rarely read, and I don't like writing.* Ouch.

CHAPTER 12

College Days

I was fed up with high school, so I started focusing on college. One thing I knew after all my trips to Birmingham was that I liked the South. The culture, the climate, and the energy had won me over completely. So the top priority on my list was getting away from the Northeast and going south for college.

The schools on my list included the University of North Carolina, North Carolina State University, Tulane University, and the University of Alabama. Though I had done well in high school, ending up with a 4.1 weighted GPA that ranked me somewhere around eighty-sixth in my class, I hadn't taken any Advanced Placement courses. That meant that I wasn't going to stand out enough purely based on my academic record.

I also had to think about tuition cost. My parents were prepared to help me pay for a portion of it, but tuition plus room and board at some of these schools was more than $50,000 a year. I would need some form of financial aid or scholarships to cover the gap. My parents and I did a lot of research and found out that Tulane had a community service scholarship that was unique among the schools I was looking at and would pay for about a third of the annual tuition. The main requirement was a personal essay describing the community service you had done. So, without ever having visited the school, I wrote my essay and applied. I have to admit, I was feeling good about my chances. I knew the type of service activities that the majority of the kids my age were doing—selling Christmas trees at the Boys and Girls Club, coaching Little League, volunteering at a food pantry, and so on. I made a bet with my dad—if I got the community service scholarship from Tulane, he would buy me a car.

I got a general acceptance letter to the school in December, and in early January I got word that I had won the scholarship. I was thrilled about the scholarship, but even more so about the car—I wanted a car more than anything. My dad wound up getting me a Mazda Tribute, which he bought from his friend, a local bartender. Note to self: never buy a car from a bartender. It turned out to be a rolling hunk of garbage and broke down four times within the first two weeks. But it was better than nothing.

With the scholarship paying about a third of the tuition, we were able to make up the remainder with the savings that my parents had stashed away, plus student loans I took out. I also got a few minor scholarships from the town of Arlington at an Awards Night that brought in another $5,000 or so.

I finally got to visit Tulane during a special event for accepted students. I was blown away by the school and by New Orleans. It was unlike anywhere I'd ever been. For a teenager especially, I think, it's like stepping into a dream. Bars. Clubs. Music festivals. Food festivals. Every band you can think of comes through New Orleans at some point. Nirvana was no longer my favorite group, but I was still really into music. My tastes were eclectic, from rock to blues to country. I was absolutely convinced New Orleans was the right place for me. Once you visit New Orleans, it's pretty hard for other college towns to compete.

My dad and I were walking down the street together during my visit, right after a violent rainstorm—they seemed to hit every day around noon—and we saw water shooting up out of the drains. We were reminded of Hurricane Katrina and the fact that New Orleans is below sea level. While it's an incredible city, it also has a painful legacy of human suffering and governmental negligence, sitting just below the surface of all the glitz.

I had a guy come up to me during that visit, while I was standing next to my dad, and ask if I wanted to go to a strip club. I told the guy I was only seventeen—and felt like an idiot when he looked at me with a bemused expression, like he was thinking, *Dude, why would you tell me that?* My dad grinned and messed with me in my already embarrassed state by saying, "I thought you were eighteen." The incident gave me my first taste of how fluid concepts like "legal drinking age" were in New Orleans.

I started at Tulane in the fall of 2012 and loved the college experience from the get-go, which was perhaps best summed up for me by the time-honored motto: work hard, play hard. I did well academically despite the proximity of Bourbon Street and the city's adult Disneyland feel. I had a great group of friends, with similar viewpoints and interests. We went to food and music festivals like the Crescent City Blues & BBQ Festival, the Tremé Creole Gumbo Festival, and the French Quarter Festival. And amusingly, it was talking about the Negro Leagues that helped me break the ice with my first girlfriend. I was at a bar during my freshman year—as I said, the idea of a legal drinking age was flexible in New Orleans, and many bars only required you to be eighteen to enter—and started talking to a girl. We did the usual, awkward first questions about where we were from and what we were doing in New Orleans. She was in the city visiting a friend at Tulane. When she told me she was from Kansas City, I responded, "Oh, that's where the Negro Leagues museum is. You ever been there?"

"Of course!" she said. The Negro Leagues Baseball Museum is a popular destination, especially for school trips.

"Well, I'm actually a Negro League baseball researcher," I said.

I'm not sure how impressed she was by this, but it got us talking, and we spent a lot of time together over the next few days. When she went back to Kansas City, we kept in touch. The next fall, she moved to New Orleans, and we dated for about a year.

While at Tulane I also helped establish a business fraternity on campus, and I became the president of it during my senior year. We brought in local business owners and entrepreneurs to speak about their work and give us advice. This was especially relevant to me, because I had kept my autograph and memorabilia business active. I'd hired a couple of guys to work for me in New York and in Boston, and in 2013, which was the end of my freshman year at Tulane, I had to pay taxes because I got a 1099 form in the mail telling me I had made more than $20,000 the previous year selling items on eBay. By my sophomore year I had more than a thousand items in my eBay store.

I also kept in touch with the Negro Leaguers I'd already befriended, continued to work on pensions, went to every reunion, and tried to locate additional players. There were major advantages to being in the South for making new and deepening old connections with Negro Leaguers. For example, while I was at Tulane, I finally got to meet a former player named Bill Stewart. I'd gotten connected to Bill a few years earlier through Herb Simpson, one of his former teammates. Bill and I had remained in touch by mail and over the phone throughout my time in high school. But since he was in his late nineties, I figured the chances were low that I'd get the opportunity to meet him in person.

Bill proved me wrong. When I met him in his home in Gretna, Louisiana, a few miles outside of New Orleans, he was one hundred years old, and in the honorable position of being the oldest known living Negro League player. Bill shared stories about his playing days and his teammates. He'd started playing professional baseball with some local teams in the New Orleans area around 1930, and eventually went on to play short stints with a number of Negro League teams including the New Orleans Black Pelicans, Portland Rosebuds, Memphis Red Sox, and Algiers Giants. He hadn't played long enough to be eligible for an MLB pension, but he had worked for the New Orleans Archdiocese for years, and fortunately had a retirement plan through them. I gave him several newspaper articles from when he played with the Memphis Red Sox; he showed me a picture of him with the Algiers Giants, and several awards he had received. I continued to stop by Bill's house periodically to catch up and chat during my time at Tulane (though I regret that I never did take him up on an offer to join him for his family's New Orleans–style Thanksgiving!).

While I was at Tulane, I also made contact with a former

Me with Bill Stewart, age 101, at Bill's home in Gretna, Louisiana, in 2014.

Negro Leaguer named Gerald Sazon. I first heard about Gerald from Freddie Battle. Freddie had played for and managed the Indianapolis Clowns for the majority of the 1960s and was full of stories. His grandkids weren't into baseball, so we talked to each other weekly via phone calls and emails for years. Whenever we talked, I always asked him if there were any new names he could remember of Negro Leaguers he'd known, no matter how obscure.

One evening in 2009, in response to my question, he told me: "Well, there was this guy, Gerald Sazon, a bit older than me, who played local ball in the DC area. He also joined the Clowns for a game or two. I don't know where he's at and I haven't seen him since the mid-sixties."

I added Sazon's name to a long list of players to look for. All signs pointed toward him living in New Orleans, but I saw one address in New Orleans, then another one several hours outside of the city. I tried contacting him at each address but didn't have any success. Finally, in 2014, I found a new address. He appeared to be residing at a local senior living center only a few miles away from the Tulane campus. I couldn't get him over the phone, so I showed up at the center with a fellow baseball enthusiast who was visiting town. We told the person at the front desk we were there to see Sazon. Several minutes later he came down and I introduced myself.

We introduced ourselves to Gerald, and I told him that Freddie Battle had given me his name back in 2009. It turned out Gerald had been displaced by Hurricane Katrina, moved several hours away for a while, and then recently returned. After we got to know each other a little, I asked him: "Is it true that you only played a handful of games with the Indianapolis Clowns in your baseball career?"

"Oh, no," he responded. "I was in my thirties and working full-time when I joined the Clowns. But I played on the New Orleans Black Pelicans and New Orleans Creoles for five seasons in the late 1940s and early '50s. Then I began producing records here in New Orleans for musicians like famed Mardi Gras Indian 'Bo' Dollis." (The Mardi Gras Indians are a legendary organization from inner-city neighborhoods in New Orleans that have developed their own style of celebrating the city's biggest holiday.)

Gerald and I hit it off. We sat around and chatted for hours, eventually becoming good friends. In an unexpected twist, one of my brothers and I were able to help him connect with a long-lost friend who lived in our hometown of Arlington, named Ron Levy. Levy wasn't a ballplayer—he sold old records at a local memorabilia show and had once played in B. B. King's band. As it turned out, long before all of that, he had lived in New Orleans and worked closely with Gerald Sazon on many albums, producing them with him and setting up international distribution. Within a week, Gerald and Ron were back to chatting like old times.

I visited Gerald a couple times each semester while I was at Tulane, and I was so honored when he came to my college graduation party. It was only appropriate that an esteemed former Negro Leaguer would be there, eating crawfish and delighting in the festivities.

While I was at Tulane, media attention on the story of me and my former ball-playing friends also continued to grow. There were two particularly big events: I was the subject of a headline profile on HBO's *Real Sports with Bryant Gumbel* during the summer after my freshman year, and then several months later, I gave a TED Talk on my exploits as a researcher. Years later, it still boggles my mind when I think about the crazy, unexpected places this hobby has taken me.

HBO's *Real Sports* is a show that my parents love, and one I grew up watching with them, so when the show reached out to do a story on me, I couldn't believe it. It was perfect because it was right before the fourth Birmingham reunion, in 2013, so the crew made a plan to meet us in Alabama to cover the reunion and talk to players, then the week after, come to Arlington to do interviews at my family's house. I started guessing right away who they might send to do the piece, and my first thought was it would be Frank Deford—he seemed to do these types of stories at the time.

We still didn't know who it would be for the first two days of the reunion. A local crew arrived in Birmingham and started filming B roll around the Redmont Hotel, but there was no big star from the show yet. Producers took aside numerous players to sit down for interviews, and *Real Sports* became the main subject of conversation in our reunion group. I am frequently pulled in a hundred different directions during the reunion, solving little problems, but that week was especially insane. At one point, two attractive middle-aged Black women showed up at the hotel and announced, "We're here for the audition."

"Excuse me?" we all said.

"We hear HBO is filming. We're here for the audition."

We had to politely tell them that there was nothing to audition for.

It wasn't until the Rickwood Classic day, in the middle of the week, that we found out who was coming to shoot the main segments for the show: Bryant Gumbel himself. He stepped out of a black Town Car at the field and we were all shocked. Here in front of us was the host of *Real Sports*, and former longtime cohost of NBC's *Today* show. He had been a regular presence in all of our living rooms for years—the players were so excited to meet him, and I was, too. Right away, Gumbel impressed us with how down-to-earth he was. He spent the day with us at the Rickwood Classic and then sat down with several guys the producers had thought would be good subjects for Gumbel to interview himself, including the irascible Frank Marsh, which was an interesting choice. But Marsh did fine, smiling and almost appearing jolly as he answered Gumbel's questions.

The following week, back in Arlington, a crew of four guys descended on my parents' house at about 8 a.m. and converted it into their studio, with lights, sound, the works. After a few hours of setup, once again, a black Town Car pulled up in front of our house and out stepped Bryant Gumbel.

My mom was almost baffled when he casually sat down and ate salsa and chips with us as we all chatted. Gumbel was just as easy to talk to in this setting, and spent about four or five hours at the house, interviewing me and my parents, hanging out in my still-messy room as I showed him my huge collection of memorabilia. He was especially stunned by my five hundred or so signed baseballs.

When the episode aired a few months later, my head almost exploded when I heard what Gumbel said about me, to a national audience, in the opening of the piece.

"His name is Cam Perron and although just eighteen, he has become one of this country's foremost authorities on baseball's old Negro Leaguers—and one of their closest friends as well," said Gumbel, as the screen filled with an image of me being hugged at Rickwood Field by former player Ernest Fann. I was touched on an even deeper level when multiple players told Gumbel in the episode that they viewed me as almost like a son—that's how close they felt to me.

The *Real Sports* piece was a moment of pride for me and all of the former Negro Leaguers who were involved. It was powerful and effective, combining facts about the Negro Leagues and their importance with a moving exploration of how meaningful it has been for these former players to finally be recognized for their contributions to the game. It had a significant added benefit, too, in that after seeing it quite a few people reached out to me with information on

Me with Bryant Gumbel filming a segment for *Real Sports*.

former Negro Leaguers, whom I was able to connect with as a result.

After the high of *Real Sports*, I have to admit that my TED Talk wasn't quite as successful.

A TED organizer contacted me during the summer of 2013, when I was going into my sophomore year of college, and invited me to speak at a conference that was taking place in New Orleans in the fall. The truth was, I had no idea what the hell a TED Talk was. But I felt like a seasoned public speaker by this time, and I accepted without hesitation.

The event was called TEDYouth and was intended to target a younger audience. It was organized directly by TED (as opposed to the omnipresent TEDx Talks that can be hosted by just about anybody). However, I knew none of this at the time. As a result, I failed to recognize the magnitude of the moment—and did very little to prepare. I didn't know that a TED Talk differed from a normal speech, that you're supposed to pose a question and look at it from different perspectives. I was given six minutes, and I spent the entire time talking about myself, yapping a mile a minute, stepping through the details of my journey to national renown.

I knew it hadn't gone well as soon as I stepped off the stage. That feeling was made even worse when I watched the actor Ashton Kutcher come up a few speakers after me and wow the crowd with his presentation. Over the next few days, I watched videos of other speakers who had been at my event. Some eventually racked up millions of page views. I, unsurprisingly, did not.

CHAPTER 13

My Old Friends

As I got older, my friendships with many former Ne[gro]
League players strengthened. The annual reunion in Birm[i]
ham was the catalyst—taking what had been phone, le[tter]
and email relationships to the next level by giving us the [op]
portunity to meet in person and spend time together. Th[ere]
were hundreds of players I got to know and befriend in t[his]
critical way, thanks to the reunions. But there were three pl[ay]
ers in particular I became especially close with over the ye[ars:]
Gil Black, Ernest Fann, and Russell Patterson. There might [be]
a sixty-year age difference between us, but these three g[uys]
are among my best friends in the world.

I'd like to let each of them tell their stories, starting w[ith]
Gilbert Black:

*I learned to play baseball in New York City, where I was born
in 1934. I lived two blocks from the Polo Grounds, where the
New York Giants played. When I was in grammar school and*

middle school, we used to sneak into the ballpark and watch the games. Those were the years of Bobby Thomson, Eddie Stanky, Buddy Kerr, Sid Gordon. In New York, there wasn't any segregation with the fans between Blacks and whites. We could sit where we wanted.

When I got older and started playing myself, we would go looking for places to play. That's when things would be segregated; there were places that whites played and places that Blacks played. I met a few Negro League ballplayers in Central Park. When I played across the street from Yankee Stadium, in Macombs Dam Park, I met a Negro League player that I think was Luis Tiant Sr., the former Red Sox pitcher Luis Tiant's father. The senior Tiant was a pitcher in the Negro Leagues for the New York Cubans. [Baseball guru Bill James ranked the elder Tiant's screwball the seventh-best of all time.] I read in a book that Tiant used to go to Macombs Park to practice his pitching for the Negro League season. I met a left-handed pitcher that looked like Tiant at Macombs, and he would ask me to catch him while he practiced his pitching. I didn't know who it was; he never told me his name. I used to skip school and meet him at Macombs. He would give me tips about pitching. I just called him "sir." But he was very impressive.

When I was about seventeen, my mother moved us up to Stamford, Connecticut. My grandfather lived there, so she sold the cleaners she owned in New York and brought us up there. I started playing baseball for the Stamford Eagles, a Black semipro team. The New Haven Indians came down to

play us; they bet a lot of their money on the game. I pitched and beat them, 1–0. After the game, they had a hard time scraping together money for the bus driver because we won all their money. A couple days later, two guys came down from New Haven looking for me. They were playing against the Hartford Chiefs, the farm team for the Boston Braves, and they wanted me to pitch for them because they had bet a lot of money on the game. My mother didn't want me to do it because I was in high school. So they told her, "Well, we'll change his name." I started that game as "Kenny Hart."

I beat the Chiefs, so the New Haven guys won a lot of money. They gave me twenty-five dollars for pitching. I was just a junior in high school at the time.

After I graduated, a sportswriter for the Stamford Advocate *called me on the phone.*

"They're having a Braves tryout up in Meriden, Connecticut. Would you like to go?" he asked.

"Yeah. I don't have a way to get there, but I'd like to go."

"If you can find somebody to drive, I'll give you the money to get there," he said.

When I got there, the manager of the Hartford Chiefs was coming out of the clubhouse and he saw me.

"Hey! I've been looking for you all year," he said. Because I had used the name Kenny Hart to pitch against them, nobody could figure out who in the world I was. Next thing I know, the Braves sent their head scout, Jeff Jones, down to Stamford to sign me. I went to spring training the next year, in Lake Forest, Georgia, their minor-league training facility.

They assigned me to West Palm Beach—but the manager of the West Palm Beach team was very prejudiced. I had one bad game and he released me. The next year I went to a tryout for the Pirates, but I got sick on the way down there because the roof flew off my car and I caught pneumonia. But that's when I heard from the Clowns. They already knew me because I pitched a game for them when they came up to Rye, New York, and I won. They handed me a uniform and I joined the Indianapolis Clowns. I was twenty-one. But I only played one year.

Choo-Choo Coleman, who went on to play for the New York Mets, he was our catcher. When I was playing third one night, a guy hit a pop-up. I went over and caught the ball in the coach's box—and Choo-Choo came running down the line and ran straight into my arm. My arm was broken; that slowed down my baseball career. The next year they called me to come back with the Clowns, but I had gotten a real good job that paid good money and I had gotten married. So I didn't go back, which was a big mistake because I had a lot of people still interested in me.

It was one of my greatest thrills to play for the Clowns. That was a famous team when I was growing up. We had so many stories. One time when we played in Biloxi, Mississippi, a police car came and drove right onto the field. It went up next to home plate and stopped. I was playing center field. The sheriff got out the car, walked past the pitcher, past the shortstop, and he came out to center field. He looked me up and down, then he shook his head. He went back to the car, got in, and left. You see, I'm a light-skinned Black. What happened was, somebody had called the Sheriff's Department and told them there was a white kid out there playing with some Black boys. When you played in the circuit of the Indianapolis Clowns, a lot of the fields had lights that weren't that bright. I'm light—my mother's father was Irish-German and my mother was Spanish—but I'm not that light.

I got great memories of that year. When our bus rolled into town, everybody would come running over to the bus, all the kids and a bunch of different people. It was a great thing; we really were superstars. But the Negro Leagues were changing, declining. Because of the major league. Why would one of these major-league teams want to get a guy out of high school and train him when they could just snatch him from the Negro Leagues? Just like they did with Ernie Banks.

Banks played two seasons with the Monarchs. When he signed with the Cubs, he just changed uniforms. He didn't go to the minor leagues or nothing like that. Hank Aaron played one year with the Clowns, before I got there. The Negro Leagues for a lot of players were the same as the major league. The players were that good. And it was an unwritten law with the major-league teams that there could only be two Blacks on a team. If you weren't an established Black player, it was hard to get on a team. A guy coming out of high school didn't have that much going for him.

One day I was sitting around with my daughter at her house in Atlanta and she asked me, "Dad, what team did you play with in the Negro Leagues?"

"The Indianapolis Clowns," I told her.

She put it on the computer somewhere, and next thing I know, I have some guy calling me on the phone and asking, "Are you Gil Black?"

"Yeah," I said.

"Well, I'm Cam," he said. "I've been looking for you for a couple years now."

And that's how I first got introduced to my friend Cam Perron. I got to talking with him and got to know him pretty well. Cam is a great kid. I could tell by the sound of his voice that he was probably a young white kid. I met him in person soon after in Birmingham. He told me about the reunions they have and he suggested I come down.

"You get down here and we'll take care of the rooms and stuff," he said.

So my niece, who is a federal judge, bought me an airline ticket and I took a plane down to Birmingham from my home in Connecticut. I got off the plane and called the hotel where we're supposed to be and the next thing I know, here comes Cam in a van with Dr. Revel. That's the first time I saw him. I got in the van with them and drove to the hotel. But before I could even get in the hotel, I ran into Reginald Howard, who also played for the Clowns. We sat there talking for a long time. It was great to get back together with the guys. I was so glad Cam invited me down. Most of the guys had such a love for the game of baseball. They might've no longer been involved in baseball professionally, but we all loved the game so much.

COMEBACK SEASON

As I've mentioned, Gil and I went on to give speeches together on the Negro Leagues at a variety of events during my senior year in high school, and we had a lot of fun traveling around the area, perfecting our two-man show.

Gilbert Black playing for the Indianapolis Clowns, 1956.

I'd been talking to Ernest Fann for years, and got the chance to spend some quality time with him at the third Birmingham reunion, since he'd recently retired from his career as a furniture salesman and finally had time to come to all of the events. We became fast friends. Fann had a long and notable baseball career. He started in the Negro Leagues with the Raleigh Tigers, spent time in the minors for affiliates of St. Louis and Kansas City, among other major-league teams, and then played in the Industrial League in Birmingham for fifteen years.

A couple things that always come up at the reunions are doubts about and challenges to the stories the players share with one another. Every hitter seemed to have had a batting average of .400, and every pitcher seemed to have a miraculous win-loss record. Players often turned to me to settle these friendly debates, because I had the best access to the thing that couldn't lie: newspaper clippings. There was one particularly memorable story about this with Ernest Fann. He told everyone about a game where he struck out nearly every player who came to bat. Players instantly doubted him. Later that night, I found a newspaper article proving every word he'd said. That's Ernest.

Here's Ernest Fann telling the story of his baseball career:

I was about eight years old when I started playing baseball, in my hometown of Macon, Georgia, where I was born on July 24, 1943. I was not exposed to racism like a lot of Black people were because my neighborhood was integrated and everybody got along. The next-door neighbor was white, and he had two daughters who were tickled to death to be out there playing stickball with Black guys. Blue Moon Odom stayed a block away. [Odom, a two-time major-league All-Star, was a right-handed pitcher with the Oakland A's team that won three consecutive World Series championships from 1972 to 1974. He was signed by the Kansas City A's upon graduation from Macon's Ballard-Hudson High School.] Our whole high school sports program was from my neighborhood in Macon.

I wasn't exposed to racism until I got into [minor-league] professional baseball. It hadn't even happened yet, before that, when I played in the Negro Leagues, for the Raleigh Tigers. I played with Raleigh in 1962, when I was eighteen, getting ready to turn nineteen. The Negro Leagues were declining by then. The thing that turned me off about playing in Raleigh was we didn't get paid. All we got was meal money—five dollars every three days. We'd play in a town, get on the bus, and drive to the next town. Wherever we could find water, even in a creek, we'd wash our uniforms and hang them on the bus while we drove to the next town.

Guys like Satchel Paige got paid. He's gonna get his money. They gave him gifts like cars, hunting equipment. He's gonna get his because he was a great pitcher and he was a showman. Josh Gibson was a great catcher; he's gonna get paid. But the regular Negro Leaguers? We didn't. The week before the season ended, we told the owner, Arthur Dove, that we were going home. He begged us for an hour and a half to stay. We felt he was making money. Every game we had, the stands were full. The teams split the gate—sixty percent to the winner, forty percent to the loser. Somebody was making money.

It wasn't all fun on the road. One time we were in the

Tennessee mountains and the bus's brakes went out. It was scary, but we had an excellent driver—he downshifted all the way to the bottom of the mountain and made sure we were safe.

I got approached by the St. Louis Cardinals and signed a contract with them toward the end of 1962. I was a catcher at the time. I batted .303 for their minor-league teams. They couldn't get me out. The Cardinals were a classy A-1 organization. But the next year they traded me to the Kansas City Athletics. That was the most racist organization in baseball back then, I hate to say it. For the first time I got exposed to racism in the worst way. They had to change their tune when they moved to Oakland [in 1968], with all them Black folks out there.

Kansas City sent me to their minor-league team in Burlington, Iowa. In the whole town, I was the only Black person there. When I went out for warm-ups, the white players told me they didn't want me to sit on the bench with them. They didn't want me to hear the racist remarks they would make. So I had to go to the bullpen and sit by myself.

One of the guys in the stands asked me, "Hey, what are you doing down here?"

I wasn't shy about telling him. "The white ballplayers didn't want me sitting on the bench," I said. A bunch of other fans heard me and they had a fit. Those people were not [racist] like that. They said they wanted to get the Kansas City organization out of their city.

Kansas City had decided they didn't want me as a catcher.

for Stockham—when you're a baseball player, they don't give you no hard jobs.

I stayed with them for fifteen years. I played until I was almost forty. I was still throwing about ninety [miles per hour] when I stopped, still bringing it.

Cam is my friend. When I first met him, I called him a little boy. But when we got together, we established a real friendship with each other. That's something that never happens, considering the differences between us. But it's because we can communicate with each other. We don't care who knows it—we're like brothers. Even though I'm a lot older, we act like brothers.

Cam was great as far as research goes. It was like he had spent his entire life researching Negro League ballplayers. He told me things about my playing days I didn't even remember. He did research on me that they put in the museum in Birmingham—you can go in there and see the window on me. Cam was enthused about the career I had. I did some things in my career he couldn't believe. He got a kick out of talking to me about when I pitched a no-hitter and struck out twenty-four batters. There's a write-up in the museum about that. Cam and I speak the same language on the history of the Negro Leagues.

The last time I saw Cam was last year at the reunion, but I just talked to him a week ago. When he and Dr. Revel come to town, I take them to a soul food restaurant called Fife's in downtown Birmingham. They eat until they can hardly walk—collard greens, neck bones, chicken. They love to go *there. When they come, they gonna find me no matter where I am. We going to the restaurant. They call me Big Dog. Dr. Revel's wife is no different—if she's with him, she's not gonna let us go by ourselves. She's going, too.*

When we all get together for the reunion, it's very important to the players. It gives us an opportunity to meet each other every year and talk about the old days. If you want to see a sight, see a bunch of Negro Leaguers talking about the old days.

Ernest and I regularly keep up by phone and text message. As he mentioned, Ernest lives in Birmingham, and every time

Ernest Fann at the Rickwood Classic game, 2018.

I go there, to this day, he insists on picking me up from the airport and taking me out to dinner.

From the beginning, when I was with Russell "Crazy Legs" Patterson, we were cool as can be. We just really hit it off from the very first reunion. Russell seemed to get me, and wanted to make sure I was treated as one of the guys. We both like to trash-talk a little bit, and tell it like it is. Whenever I see Russell, I know I'm going to have a good time.

Here's Russell "Crazy Legs" Patterson, describing his baseball career, and our friendship:

I was born in Savannah, Georgia, on April 27, 1939. I didn't really start playing baseball until I was about twelve or thirteen. Because of racism, we didn't have a Little League or anything like that. A guy from a different part of town asked my mother if I could play with him. I was just one of the guys, out there playing. I had no idea I was any good. I didn't even have a glove. I took a brown paper bag and made it into a glove so the ball wouldn't sting when I caught it. I'd just run in the outfield and catch everything. It was just something to do. I had a great childhood, great parents. My parents weren't strict—they'd let us do what we wanted to do, until we did something wrong. I didn't have my own glove until I was sixteen or seventeen. My brother bought it for me. Until then I would borrow gloves. Since I was a lefty, I was always playing with a right-handed glove that

I turned around. I didn't have a lefty glove until I had my own glove.

Being a left-hander helped me in everything. Even when I played basketball. Everybody thought it was odd. Back in the fifties and sixties, if you were left-handed everybody tried to change you to right-handed. Especially down South. They always thought if you were left-handed, you were one of the devil's children—stuff like that. Like something was wrong with you. But my parents never tried to change me.

I played first base, pitcher, and outfield. Those were the only positions you could play if you were a lefty. They used to call me Little Lefty 'cause I was about five-eight or five-nine, 157 pounds. I kept getting tryouts for the major league, but it was plain old racism that kept me out. They would tell us to our face that they already had enough colored or Cuban ballplayers. Every time we would go to one of the camps, they would come up with a different story for why they didn't sign us. But the reality was they didn't want us to dominate and take the white guys' jobs. It's just as simple as that. When I played first base, the first thing they told me was I was too showboat. I told that man straight to his face, "Hey, I'm good. That's the way I play. Ain't nothing going by me."

But they didn't like that. I don't even know what they meant about me being a showboat. Wasn't anything flashy about the way I caught the ball. I'm not going to look like a statue out there. I made the plays and went about my business. I didn't play around. When I was an outfielder, I had a BB of an arm. When I threw the ball in, it was in. Matter of fact, sometimes I would let the guy run a little bit and then fire it in to get him. But I was never cocky! They would always find something wrong with us. Always. There was a white kid who was trying out next to me for Detroit who couldn't catch a drop of water if he threw a bucket up in the air, but Detroit signed him to a minor-league contract. I don't know where he went and how long he stayed, but they sure did sign him.

I got sent home both years I went to camp. One year a guy down there in Florida told me to my face, "I don't care how good you get, I'm gonna tell you straight out, you better learn something else 'cause you are not gonna play no major-league ball."

Simple. They didn't beat around the bush with it. It was just racism, prejudice. That's what it was. That's why we had the Negro Leagues, 'cause a lot of us can play ball. But they would throw some excuse at us. You hit a line drive and the guy catches the ball, but they'd say to you, "You didn't run to first base fast enough." You didn't do this. You didn't do that. Always some excuse. Then they were trying to tell me I was too small. Willie Mays, Hank Aaron, who played on the Clowns before me—they're not that big. When I was seventeen, they put a radar gun on me and I was throwing ninety miles per hour, with movement. This scout from the Yankees told me I had the best screwball he had ever seen. Another guy from the Cardinals said I had the best pickoff move he had ever seen, me being left-handed. There were other guys in the majors who were smaller than me, guys who threw no-hitters. Go look at the history. But it didn't matter. Same thing today, *making excuses. When a white coach does something, he's got the greatest mind in the world. But a Black coach? Oh, he's not smart enough to do nothing. It's just pitiful.*

I ended up playing a full season with the Clowns in 1960. I was supposed to play with them in '61. By '60 and '61, the Clowns were the only team that was getting paid on time because the league was failing. And we had our own bus. But my sister who lived in New Jersey told me there was a team up there that needed ballplayers and they were paying good. I went up there and I was getting $150 a month to play, plus $2 a day to eat with. Then there was the betting. [There was a betting culture in some parts of the Negro Leagues, with owners and local attendees connected in various ways to bookies.] Guys would tell me, "Look, if you pitch and win the ballgame, you could get ten percent." I was seriously making three hundred or four hundred dollars a week playing in Jersey. I'd play during the week and then pitch for somebody else on the weekend. It didn't bother me. But I should have stayed longer with the Clowns.

I met Cam for the first time when he was just fifteen, at the first reunion in Birmingham. I heard some of the guys talking about the little white kid this, the little white kid that. They were complaining about him, saying how could a white kid tell Black people what to do. I didn't like hearing that. I told them he's a little white kid that's actually leading a bunch of old Black men to success. He helped my career in so many ways. Not just me but a lot of them. I talked to Bryant Gum-

Russell Patterson *(top row, fifth from left)* with his Indianapolis Clowns teammates, 1960.

bel on HBO. I'm in three different books. I can go speak any-where now; people are calling me to speak. All because of him. I think he's great—and I tell that to everybody. All these guys are getting their pension money because of Cam. I didn't stay four years so I'm not getting the pension. I wish I had. But I'm living great, so it's okay.

His mother brought him to the reunion that first year, in 2010, but after him and I got together, his mother said, "That's it—you go down there with Crazy Legs." And that's what he did. We been doing that ever since, rooming together every year. I only missed one year, because my knee swolled up and the doctor wouldn't let me drive and my wife

229

wouldn't let me drive. But I love coming to the reunion and
talking to the guys about the game.

Rooming with Russell at the reunion has become a tradition. We've done it every year since the second reunion in 2011, except for that year he couldn't make it because of his knee. I guess I could get my own room, but I enjoy the camaraderie of spending time with my friend. Sometimes we'll hang out in the lobby talking to guys until the wee hours, or we'll go back up to the room and laugh together over some comedy special until two in the morning—and then wake up early the next day to dive back into the reunion activities.

Russell even vacationed with my family. It happened in 2010, after we met at the first reunion. Later that summer when my family took a vacation in Myrtle Beach, South Carolina, I called Russell up since he didn't live far away.

"Hey, Russell, I'm coming to South Carolina. Do you want to come by?" I asked him.

He said yes, and we settled on the idea of going to a Myrtle Beach Pelicans minor-league baseball game. My parents didn't even really know about it. When I told my family we were all going to a baseball game with Russell, though, they loved the idea. We didn't do many family vacations and my parents weren't big planners, so they were up for anything.

The game got rained out, so we wound up just having dinner and hanging out with Russell at this outdoor mall. Russell knew my mom from the reunion. He didn't really know my dad or my brothers—though I'm sure he had talked to my dad once or twice before on the phone. A lot of the players that would call all the time, like Russell, would get to know my parents when I wasn't home.

Russell came out again the next day for the rescheduled minor-league game. It was funny because I'd already made plans with Cowboy Atterbury to come to the game that day. Although Cowboy is originally from South Carolina, he now lives in Virginia. When I told him where we would be on vacation, he didn't hesitate to say he'd get in his car and drive eight hours to meet us at the game—which was absolutely crazy for a seventy-something-year-old guy. But that's Cowboy.

So I wound up getting Russell, Cowboy, and my entire family to all go to the Myrtle Beach Pelicans game together. We had such a great time. Cowboy got us in for free with some special gold pass he had from playing so many years in the minor leagues. After we got there, I decided to sneak away to the PA booth to talk to the announcer.

"Hey, I wanted to let you know that we have two Negro League legends in the audience tonight," I said. "I wondered if maybe we can do a little recognition of them on the loudspeaker, give them some credit." The guys in the booth were enthusiastic about it.

In between innings in the middle of the game, the announcer said, "We just wanted to call your attention to two Negro League legends in the stands tonight."

Russell and Cowboy were very surprised. They stood up

From left: Russell "Crazy Legs" Patterson, James "Cowboy" Atterbury, and me at the Myrtle Beach Pelicans minor-league game in August 2010.

and waved to the crowd. They took a bow with all the loud cheers coming their way. I could tell they were pleased.

I think one of the main reasons that Gil, Ernest, Russell, Cowboy, and other players I've grown close with over the years enjoy spending time with me is because they don't get a chance to talk about their playing days much in their day-to-day lives. For the most part, their wives have heard it all before. The kids and grandkids don't seem to want to dive in deep, especially when they're young.

So, in many cases, I'm the only person who remains genuinely interested in hearing about their exploits on the diamond more than a half century ago. I got that sense from the very first time that we talked on the phone; they had a lot of memories and stories—some hilarious, others painful—that had built up over the years, and that they needed to talk about. That's why some of them would call me three or four times a week, or drive hundreds of miles to get together. They just wanted to talk to somebody who cared.

CHAPTER 14

The Comeback

In August 2015, during my junior year at Tulane, I made that long trip by train from New Orleans to Birmingham for the ribbon cutting ceremony of the Negro Southern League Museum. It had been nearly eight years since I'd first made personal contact with a former Negro League player, John "Mule" Miles. Over that span of time, my entire world had changed.

As I described in the prologue, the museum's opening was a day of culmination and celebration. After years of talking about it, Dr. Revel and Chef Clayton had finally made their dream a reality. The two of them, and me as well, were listed on the museum's website under the header "Meet the Researchers." We didn't bother with more formal titles, since that wasn't what this was about.

What mattered was that all of the work we'd done to recognize Negro League players was being enshrined in a museum with top-notch exhibits, educating the world about what these

235

men were able to do when bigotry and hate tried to deny them a place to display their talents. A big section of Dr. Revel's private collection of artifacts and memorabilia was now inside, on permanent loan. It was almost surreal to me to stand in front of the stately two-story building at 120 16th Street, right next to the AA Birmingham Barons home stadium. It was tangible evidence of the progress we had made over the years. The mayor of Birmingham cut the ribbon with the former players, including Ernest Fann, Joseph Marbury, Joe Elliott, Oliver "Son" Ferguson, the now ninety-seven-year-old Roosevelt Jackson, Clinton "Tiny" Forge, Merritt "Pee Wee" Stoves, Archie "Dropo" Young, Earl Harry, Tony Lloyd, Ferdinand Rutledge, Al Holt, Cleophus Brown, Henry Elmore, Earnest Harris, Willie Walker, John Mitchell, Jake Sanders, and Sam Brunner. Just like that, the museum was open.

The "wall of balls" was the highlight for most of the players, thrilling them to no end. Every baseball that we had acquired over the years signed by a Negro Leaguer was carefully set in a massive, glass-encased display. Players were walking in and immediately searching for their ball. They'd come to me in alarm when they couldn't find it.

"Cam, where's my baseball?" asked Earl Harry. Earl had played for the New York Black Yankees. He had a toothpick in his mouth, as always.

When I helped him locate the ball, a look of relief crossed his face, and the same look crossed all the other players' faces when I helped them locate theirs. It was like their place in history had been assured: when they were gone, they knew

Clinton "Tiny" Forge, formerly of the Detroit Stars, and me, in front of the Negro Southern League Museum's "wall of balls," after the ribbon cutting ceremony on August 28, 2015.

at least their baseball would be left behind, attesting to their participation in these historic leagues.

Chef Clayton and Dr. Revel have a few closing reflections that they'd like to share about our years of work together, our relationships, and the museum.

Here's Chef Clayton looking back on our work together:

Dr. Revel and I met for the first time when he first started coming to Birmingham, almost twenty years ago. He and I got together and found out we were both really involved with the Negro Leagues. A few years later, I got a telephone call from this little young guy. He was about thirteen or fourteen, and he called me because he had read somewhere doing research that I was a batboy for the Birmingham Black Barons at Rickwood Field a long time ago. It was Cam Perron.

When Cam came to the first reunion, his mama brought him down because he was too young to come by himself. I got a chance to meet his mother; we had a reception at my house. We all had a fantastic time. When he came the next year, he stayed with me. I invited him down and he stayed at my house. My wife fell in love with him. She just loved her some Cam Perron. He was just such a nice little kid. There was something about this little young white boy who was in love with the Negro Leagues. It was so unusual. And he knew everything about the Negro Leagues. He knew all the players, the ones that were forgotten about, the ones who had died. He had a photographic memory, going back and talking about people I remembered when I was a little boy. It's just something you don't find. After a few days at my house, Cam said he wanted to stay in the hotel. I understood. He was so happy being down there right in the midst of everything.

Cam always had on this backpack. He'd walk around with his backpack and little short britches with those skinny legs. He was all over the place, gathering information, taking pictures of the guys. One year I said, "Cam, instead of taking pictures of the guys, you have to start taking pictures with the guys."

So I would stand there with the guys and he would take a picture, then I would go get the camera from him and take a picture of him with the guys. Cam got a picture of every Negro League player that even thought about coming to Birmingham. He's got thousands of pictures. And he has very easy access to them. When somebody calls me and asks if I have a picture of a certain player, it would take me an hour to try to find it. Cam would have it in a few seconds and zip it off to me.

Cam and I became very close. I would check on him. Me, Dr. Revel, and Crazy Legs [Russell Patterson] treated him just like our son. When he went to Tulane, I told him, "It's wild down there in Louisiana! You gotta call me a couple times a week to let me know how you doing." And he did.

He helped out quite a bit in getting the information together for the museum. We went through so many changes over the years, at different times dealing with four mayors of Birmingham. Every one of them had different ideas about a Negro League museum. We almost got there with Mayor Larry Langford, but it didn't happen before he left office. When the next occupant of the seat, Mayor William Bell, came into office, the plans were already in place. I'm so pleased it finally got built.

And now, here are Dr. Revel's thoughts about what we've accomplished in our work together:

When we began, we were told that there were 275 living ballplayers who had played in the Negro Leagues. Since the Cen-

ter for Negro League Baseball Research has been in existence, we have found over 750 more ballplayers. In addition to that, we found another 500-plus that played some level of Black baseball—whether regional ball, Florida Coast Negro League, Texas Colored League, or maybe for an independent team like the Indianapolis Clowns. We have greatly expanded the idea of how many are out there.

Much of our work culminated in the establishment of the museum in Birmingham to display the artifacts and tell the story. There are 1,658 autographed baseballs from players on display there. Cam or I have interviewed all but six of them. We have more than fifty original uniforms from the Negro Leagues. We have over a hundred bats that have been used in the Negro Leagues. We've got historically important pieces, such as the McAllister Trophy, which was for the Colored Championship of the South in the early 1900s. We have the American Cup that the Negro League All-Stars won in Cuba. We have Satchel Paige's uniform, Willie Wells's uniform. We have the oldest known contract from Negro League baseball.

Last year, in 2019, I was thrilled when Cam held the reunion himself. I couldn't go because I was out of the country. It was astounding to me to reflect back on a relationship that began when he was a middle schooler, calling me for information, and that has grown to the point where we are friends and colleagues, despite a forty-five-year difference in our ages. I'm seventy years old now, and it is so gratifying for me to know *that when I pass on, Cam will run the Center for Negro League Baseball Research. He'll be responsible for the museum. Cam will take over from where I left off. As a matter of fact, for the last five years I consider Cam as having been running the Center for Negro League Baseball Research with me.*

I feel so pleased that I have somebody to carry on my legacy, after more than thirty years of doing this work. It's truly a remarkable story. And you know, Cam owns his own business now. He's got a phenomenal head for business; his company is very successful. The time he takes away from his business is money that he's not making for his business. Cam does this because he sees a real importance to it.

I find it fascinating. I'm a rehab doctor; I deal with people at their worst—folks that are train wrecks, to be honest with you. It is so refreshing when you see people, especially young people, that are doing things that are good, and doing them just because they're good. It's not about "what's in it for me?"

Every player we find, we're able to document and preserve their history. With the signed baseballs that we get, that we love so much, that's the first thing that the ballplayers want to see when they come to the museum. They point and say, "Oh! I signed that ball for Doc thirty years ago!" Or "I signed that ball for Cam ten years ago when he sent a box to me in the mail! I didn't have a clue why he was asking me to do it!"

The values I see in Cam just really make me proud—proud that he's my friend, proud that he's my colleague, proud that he will carry on the work that I've done, that he and I have done together, and he's doing everything all for the right reasons. Cam loves the thrill of the hunt. He loves getting on the computer and asking, Okay, I know this guy's still alive— where was he at this date? Where was he at that day? *And he's so sincere and he makes friends with so many people, everybody loves and respects him. He's doing some remarkable work.*

When I think back over the years, how much I've grown, how much things have changed, I come across a memory. There was one unforgettable night that directly involved Chef Clayton. It happened during the third reunion. Chef Clayton decided to put me on "car duty," which on this night meant driving a huge, forty-person commercial van to ferry players back and forth from a juke joint, as many of the players called it—basically a bar with music and dancing.

I should say that Chef Clayton is a—how can I say it nicely—*forceful* presence. Some might say *pushy*. He tells you to do things and expects them to be done.

He looked at me and said, "Cam, you got this, right?"

I was incredulous. "Chef, I literally got my license a year ago. I can't drive a forty-person commercial van!"

He shook his head.

"Nah, you gotta do it, you gotta do it," he said.

So I did it. I pulled the van out onto the Alabama highway at one in the morning, transporting dozens of drunk baseball players all yelling directions at me.

"Yeah, Cam, you're good to merge! You're good to merge!" they hollered from the back.

I was terrified. I was essentially driving a bus. There I was, trying to stave off a panic attack as I navigated the roadways. But somehow, I made it through the night without side-swiping anything or anybody. It reminded me to believe in myself, like Chef Clayton did, like these players did. It made me feel that I had what it takes to help people. It made me feel that I could do anything. In a nutshell, that's what my experience of getting to know Negro League players, organizing reunions, and working on pensions over all these years has done. From the time I was in daycare, I always wanted to be treated like an adult. These experiences turned me into one.

A lot has happened in my life over the last few years.

In 2017, Bryant Gumbel and *Real Sports* returned to do an update on our story. At the end of the piece, Gumbel reported about how I'd gotten a job after graduating from college with the William Morris Endeavor talent agency in Hollywood, as an assistant to one of the agents. I was helped with that by a veteran Hollywood screenwriter, Gene Hong, who saw the original *Real Sports* piece and was impressed by my drive and hustle. At the end, Gumbel said that Hong was trying to give my story a true Hollywood ending by turning it into a movie—an effort that is still in the works.

At William Morris Endeavor, I started out in the mailroom,

literally. I sorted letters, delivered packages, and picked up food, all while wearing a suit and getting paid minimum wage. When assistants—the next step up—were sick or out of town, mailroom staff would cover their desks. One day, I was assigned to cover the desk for an agent named Bethany Dick, who I soon found out was the sole L.A. agent covering speaking engagements. I told her it was good luck, because I actually had relevant experience in the field. We hit it off, and a week later I was her full-time assistant. I stayed at WME for about a year, and helped book paid speaking gigs for a variety of authors, politicians, actors, and influencers, at colleges, corporations, conferences, and charity events.

I had kept up my memorabilia and autographs business all throughout college, and continued to do so while I was at WME. One night, I was out at a bar in L.A. with some friends my age. Everyone was worrying about their student loans and how long the debt would be hanging over their heads. I chimed in.

"I've got about forty thousand to pay back," I said. "But I'll have it done in the next six months."

One girl stared at me.

"No way!" she said.

I nodded. "I'll have it wiped out in six months."

I was right. I had a good Christmas season that year. By January, the loans were all gone.

In the process, I realized that I was not only making more money through my memorabilia business than at WME, I was getting more satisfaction from it, too. I enjoyed being my own boss. So I took a risk, left WME, and turned the memorabilia business into my full-time job. I hired a couple of freelancers. I brokered autograph signings with athletes and celebrities. I flipped autographed baseballs and movie posters on eBay, Amazon, and with auction houses. And I grew the business bit by bit. I'm proud to say that it's still my full-time job today, and I'm still in L.A., doing well.

My parents remain in Arlington, and my younger brothers are now in college. I visit Boston when I can, and try to catch a Red Sox game or a concert.

Dr. Revel, Chef Clayton, the players, and I still come together at the reunions. It feels like home. Every person in town seems to know who we are, from the hotel employees to the city officials to the baseball players. The schedule of events remains pretty much the same from year to year. But the faces are slowly changing.

When I first started communicating with ballplayers more than a decade ago, the majority of the guys I was talking to were still getting around pretty well. Over the years, I've seen a decline. People who didn't have any health problems when we first met are now suffering from various health conditions. There really aren't any young guys left among the former players. If the youngest Negro Leaguer was sixteen or seventeen in 1963, he would be seventy-four or so now.

Sadly, every year guys pass away. In another two decades, there may not be any living former Negro League players left. Well over a third of the players who joined us at the first reunion in 2010 are now gone. Carl Long, who sold Negro

League gear out of his trunk at the first reunion, died in 2015. Bill Bethea, the first player I made a baseball card for, died in 2017. So did Bill Stewart, my friend in New Orleans, at age 104. But before Bill passed away, he traveled 350 miles to Birmingham for a reunion event in 2015, toured the museum, saw his signed ball on the "wall of balls," and was treated like a star by the other players. In 2018, we lost three great players: Joe Elliott, whom I was so proud of helping to get a pension; Jaycee Casselberry, who used to stay up at the reunions drinking beer into the early hours of the morning with me and his former roommate Russell Patterson; and Roosevelt Jackson, who passed away at the age of one hundred. Bob Mitchell, who did so much work advocating for his fellow players, died in 2019.

That makes me even more intent on trying to ensure that these guys not only get their due right now, but that they have a great time in the process. I want them to experience every sort of comeback that they possibly can, while they can, no matter how late it is in the season of their lives—to know for a fact that their stories matter, their memories will be preserved, and to get whatever money is owed to them by MLB. It's really been hitting me in the last few years because family members of players have started asking me to write eulogies for these men, my friends. As I flip through pictures and images in my head, trying to find the perfect words to encapsulate their lives and careers, I think about them telling me how crucial these later years have been to them. In talking to their relatives, it gets emphasized over and over how much the players enjoyed being recognized at the end, getting to know us, reconnecting with their former teammates, coming to reunions. It makes me feel right about the work we've been doing, gives me a sense of gratification. I know that I was able to help provide players with some joy at the end. It never could have made up for the years of neglect, for their nation's hate and fear, which kept many of them from enjoying the kind of professional baseball careers—and financial rewards—that would have been commensurate with their talents. But it was more than something, to bring baseball back into their lives after a half century, to tell them that they mattered, that what they did was important. I can easily conjure up an image of each of their faces, the smile beaming brightly, lighting up the room. I know that when they are with one another—reliving their former careers, throwing taunts and tall tales back and forth, the laughter rising up from their bellies—for those shining moments, all is right in their world. It's all good.

At the Rickwood Classic on May 30, 2018.

Front row, from left: Me, Russell Patterson, Senator Doug Jones, Mayor Randall Woodfin, Henry Elmore, Clayton Sherrod, Layton Revel

Second row, from left: W. James Cobbin, Anne Cobbin, Leo Westbrook, Dennis Biddle, Eugene Scruggs

Third row, from left: Clinton Johns, Donald Woods, Virgie Woods, Unknown, Reginald Howard

Fourth row, from left: Unknown, Gilbert Black, Jaycee Casselberry

Acknowledgments

First and foremost, I must reiterate the enormous gratitude I owe to the countless former Negro League baseball players who took the time to answer my letters and phone calls over the years. These men have welcomed me into their lives through an unparalleled display of generosity and hospitality despite the vast difference in our ages and backgrounds. They have shared their wealth of knowledge and personal experiences with me, and substantially shaped the person that I am today, making a lasting impact on my values, knowledge, personality, and outlook on life. They also became my friends. For all of this, I am forever grateful. While many of them have passed on, the wisdom they shared with me is still very much alive.

In particular:

Reuben Smartt, thank you for sending me $2 bills after reviewing my report card, and pushing me to always take my schoolwork seriously. I miss your yearly Christmas cards— they were exceptional.

ACKNOWLEDGMENTS

Bob Mitchell, you gave me the best trade I've ever made: autographs for As in school. You opened up my eyes to the struggles many of your fellow Negro League players faced, and the downstream effects that continued to shape their realities later in life. You also introduced me to the pensions—an opportunity to help some players get a bit of financial justice. Thank you for all of it.

Freddie Battle, thank you for your frequent reminders about the prime importance of family and relationships in life, and the happiness they bring. And thank you for your advice on girlfriends, long before I ever had one.

Bill Bethea, thank you for emphasizing the importance of being a kind and thoughtful person, giving people a chance, giving back to those around you, putting others first, and never asking for anything in return. I wish I could have met you in person.

Irvin Castille, you began encouraging me to write a book when I was thirteen years old, even sending me a list of possible book titles. I never thought it would be a reality, but now, here it is. I wish you could have read it. I'm so glad to have met you and called you a friend.

I'd also like to thank several additional players for their critical contributions to this book. Ernest Fann, Eugene Scruggs, Reginald Howard, Butch Haynes, Cowboy Atterbury, Gilbert Black, Leo Westbrook, Russell Patterson, and Gerald Sazon all graciously told their stories. While some of your stories didn't make it onto these pages directly, you all enriched this book in the deepest and most important way. Everyone who reads it should know how incredible each of you are, as baseball players, and as people.

I'd like to thank my family, especially my parents, Lauren and Dan, for driving me around to memorabilia shows, auctions, and autograph signings, and turning a blind eye to stealing their stamps for sending letters through the mail. Without their support and encouragement of my unique interests, I'd be nowhere. Ryan and Jack, thank you for your tagging alongside me over the years. Grandpa Joe and Grandma Dot, I can't thank you enough for taking me to antique stores and festivals as a child, and opening my eyes up to the vast world of collectibles. And thank you, Grandma Rita, for giving me cash instead of gift cards for my birthdays and holidays, so I could spend my money on collectibles.

Beyond my family, I owe a great deal of gratitude to the collectors who have provided me with so much knowledge, insight, and know-how about the world of memorabilia, allowing me to turn my collecting hobby into the full-time business that I operate today. Thank you, Peter, owner of the Card Dog, for treating me like an adult and a true collector from the start. Phil Chiaramonte, I cannot thank you enough for giving me a chance to be part of your team at Vintage Sports Promotions, allowing me to work with and stand alongside dozens of former professional athletes when I was just a teen. Thank you as well for your mentorship and guidance as I began to navigate the business of memorabilia shows and flipping collectibles. Additional shout-outs to Tom Killeen, Ryan McClanahan, Bob Ward, and Peter D'Amico for educating me on the collectibles market at various card shows and auction houses. And thank you to Hall's Nostalgia, for hosting memorabilia auctions in my hometown that allowed me to submerse myself in the endlessly fascinating world of memorabilia and auctions.

As my specific interest in the Negro Leagues deepened, I was guided by certain organizations and people for whom I am grateful. Thank you to the NLBPA forum, which is gone from the internet, but not forgotten. Jay Gross at SportsCollectors.Net, thank you for creating an invaluable community for through-the-mail autograph collectors. Wayne Stivers, thank you for answering my hundreds of poorly written emails as a teen asking you for players' addresses and contact information, and to answer my research questions. Thank you to Stanley Glenn, Bob Motley, John Miles, Herb Simpson, and dozens of other Negro League legends whom I first wrote to in my early days of collecting at age twelve. Your welcoming responses and detailed histories of your careers took me down a path I had never seen coming.

Dr. Layton Revel, Dr. Linda Revel, Chef Clayton Sherrod, and Sharon Sherrod, thank you for welcoming me into your lives, and taking me under your wing. Working with you each and every year to create the Negro League reunion has been one of the greatest experiences of my life. Dr. Revel, your mentorship—the encouragement and knowledge that you have shared with me—has been life changing. Chef Clayton, it's been a true pleasure having you by my side over the years

ACKNOWLEDGMENTS

and being by yours, hearing your stories, and working with you to create the iconic tradition of the reunion. Dr. Revel and Chef, you gave me the great gift of treating me as a peer from the time I was thirteen, and we haven't looked back since.

HBO and Bryant Gumbel, I cannot thank you enough. Gene Hong and Donna Gigliotti, you recognized my story and connected me with Simon & Schuster, which made this a book a reality. Gene, thank you as well for sending me that blind Facebook message back in 2013 that started it all, for bringing me out to Los Angeles, and helping me get my first job out of college.

To Nick Chiles, my cowriter, thank you for helping me reconstruct my story in book form. It was a pleasure to work with you through countless interviews and phone calls deconstructing and revisiting the many moments in my past, and helping me piece them into written form. Also, thank you to Tabitha Binner for your insight and recommendations throughout the many edits of the book.

I must express my sincere gratitude to Hank Aaron for contributing a foreword to this book. Having a true idol of mine take the time to read the book, acknowledge my work, and share his personal story and insights has been a dream come true. Hank, as a young baseball player and fan, I collected your cards, and submersed myself in the history of your career. You have always been my all-time favorite player. I cannot thank you enough. My heartfelt thanks are also due to Bob Hope for connecting me and Nick with Hank, and making the foreword a reality.

ACKNOWLEDGMENTS

I am deeply grateful for the team at Gallery Books, who took an interest in my story. Thank you to Gallery's editorial director Aimée Bell for believing in the book from the start, and publisher Jennifer Bergstrom for agreeing and making it a reality. Shout-out to Jessica Roth for being an incredible publicist (and huge sports fan), and Bianca Salvant for all of her amazing work on marketing.

Max Meltzer, I cannot thank you enough. Your guidance, leadership, and editing has been phenomenal. You've done an outstanding job working with me from the ground up to make this book what it has become; I truly could not have written this book without your guidance. And thank you to all of the production staff who were responsible for turning these words into a beautiful, finished book: managing editor Caroline Pallotta, production editor Sherry Wasserman, production manager Mike Kwan, copyeditor Rick Willett, and designer Alexis Minieri.

An additional and final shout-out is due to the City of Birmingham, Alabama, for its continuous support of the former players of the Negro Leagues, embracing our annual reunion, and funding the construction of the Negro Southern League Museum. While the building of the museum has been important to me, I know that it has also meant much more to the hundreds of players and family members than I could ever put in words. Thank you for creating a museum that will live to tell the story of the history of the Negro Leagues and its players, long after they are gone.

Photography Credits

Courtesy of Cam Perron: Pages 6, 26, 44, 93, 120, 144, 156, 187, 202, 208, 224, 232, 248

Courtesy of Lauren Perron: Pages 11, 139

Courtesy of the Ernest C. Withers Gallery: Page 53

Courtesy of Getty Images: Page 72

Courtesy of Dr. Layton Revel: Page 113

Courtesy of the Center for Negro League Baseball Research: Pages 141, 176

Courtesy of Butch Haynes: Page 161

Courtesy of Eugene Scruggs: Page 169

Courtesy of James Atterbury: Page 185

Courtesy of Gilbert Black: Page 217

Courtesy of Cam Perron and Shayla Nicole: Page 237

Public Domain/Uncredited: Pages viii, 68, 172, 229